Following at a Distance

A LENTEN STUDY FOR ADULTS

Following
at a Distance

KIMBERLY DUNNAM REISMAN

ABINGDON PRESS / Nashville

FOLLOWING AT A DISTANCE:
A LENTEN STUDY FOR ADULTS

Library of Congress Cataloging-in-Publication Data

Reisman, Kimberly Dunnam, 1960-
  Following at a distance : a Lenten study for adults / Kimberly Dunnam Reisman.
    p. cm.
  ISBN 0-687-34550-2 (alk. paper)
  1. Lent--Prayer-books and devotions--English. I. Title.

BV85.R467 2005
242'.34--dc22

2004024366

05 06 07 08 09 10 11 12 13 14 — 10 9 8 7 6 5 4 3 2 1

MANUFACTURED IN THE UNITED STATES OF AMERICA

To my parents,

MAXIE and JERRY DUNNAM

who have been for me a model
of what it means to follow in the Jesus way
never at a distance,
always close to the fire

Contents

Acknowledgments

I would like to thank the members of the Ginghamsburg Worship Team in Tipp City, Ohio, and the folks at Lumicon Digital Productions and Midnight Oil Productions for their creativity and dedication to providing resources for worship and spiritual growth. Jesus said, "From everyone to whom much has been given, much will be required" (Luke 12:48, NRSV). These capable individuals have taken Jesus' words to heart, sharing from the bounty of their gifts, talents, and resources in order to provide others with relevant tools to spread the good news in challenging, dynamic, and life-changing ways.

Introduction

As my ministry has unfolded, I have come to realize that while those of us who live in the United States enjoy the privilege of worshiping without fear of reprisal, that privilege has contributed to a profound complacency in our faith experience. For many of us, the very ease with which we are able to attend worship blocks us from recognizing the hard work and risks involved in being a follower of Jesus. Believing faith to be a risk-free endeavor, we shy away from the hard work of the soul, and thus we frequently miss out on the deeply joyful and life-changing experience of being in a dynamic relationship with Jesus Christ.

It's not that we do not desire to follow Jesus. We want to follow, but we don't always want to follow too closely. It's safer to follow at a distance, never going deeper in our faith than surface religious activity; never stepping close to the fire where we might be recognized, where we will stand out because of the way we live and the commitments we make. We are like Peter, who on the night Jesus was arrested, stood in the courtyard awaiting news of Jesus' fate. He lurked in the shadows away from the fire, trying to be invisible, trying to avoid too close a connection with the one who had changed him to his very core.

Several years ago on Palm Sunday, my congregation opened the worship service with these words:

Palm Sunday, The Lenten journey continues, this time on the final path toward Jerusalem, carefully chosen palm branches paving the way for the Master. To be there in person was to have to choose. To choose how close to get to him. To choose how many hosannas to shout in his favor. To choose how long to stay awake in the garden. To choose how much money to take in return for your soul. To choose how close to get to the fire before the rooster crows and you realize it's

11

just too hot. We settle for the safety of following from a distance rather than get burned. Yet we come here today to risk being right up in the center of activity. To choose the place right next to Jesus.

(*Handbook for Multi-Sensory Worship*, by Kim Miller; Abingdon Press, 1999; page 59)

This season, as we begin our Lenten journey together, we will be faced with those same questions. How close will we get? How many hosannas will we shout? How long will we stay awake? How close will we get to the fire before the rooster crows?

Some time ago, Garth Brooks recorded a song entitled "Standing Outside the Fire," in which he sings about how life becomes a matter of simply trying to survive rather than an experience of truly living, if you are standing outside the fire. God did not create us for mere survival. When God became human in Jesus, it was with the promise of abundant life, a life of radical transformation and deep meaning. It is my prayer that this study will challenge you to move toward that promised transformation by stepping out of the shadows and into the light and heat of the fire, by choosing the place right next to Jesus, by following him not at a distance but by his side.

How Close Will You Get?

If any of you wants to be my follower, you must put aside your selfish ambition, shoulder your cross daily, and follow me.

Luke 9:23 (NLT)

ollowing Jesus, *truly* following him, is never easy. There are risks, unexpected twists and turns, surprises and events that we never dreamed could happen. There are moments when following seems meaningful, full of excitement and joy. However, there are other times, times of difficulty, even danger, when we become discouraged and afraid, and things don't seem to be turning out at all the way we thought they would.

The apostle Peter experienced this same sense of struggling as he followed Jesus. Peter is one of my favorite people in the Bible because he reminds me of so many Christ followers, a searcher with a good heart who stumbles but tries to follow as best as he can; someone always open to growing in his relationship with Jesus, even if that growth involves some pain. Peter was full of emotion, giving himself completely to Jesus at one moment, but then fearfully retreating from Jesus the next. He boldly declared his belief that Jesus was the Messiah (Matthew 16:16), yet he turned around and questioned and chastised Jesus for talking about the suffering that lay on the horizon: "Heaven forbid, Lord. . . . This will never happen to you!" (Matthew 16:22, NLT). Peter was thoroughly genuine in all his responses, even those that were bumbling and inappropriate. When he witnessed the astonishing event of Jesus talking with Moses and Elijah on the mountain, all he could think to do was to offer to build shrines, places for each of them to live (Matthew 17; Mark 9; Luke 9). Another time, when Jesus offered to wash Peter's feet, a common way of expressing one's hospitality and servanthood in those days, Peter refused, feeling himself to be completely unworthy. When Jesus responded that it was necessary in order for Peter to be a part of him, Peter's love poured forth: "Lord, not my feet only but also my hands and my head!" (John 13:9, NRSV). Peter genuinely desired to follow Jesus, even if he didn't always know exactly what that meant; and he was willing to offer his entire self, with all of his shortcomings, knowing somehow that Jesus had created safe space between them.

Jesus understood Peter. He knew how truly human Peter was. Jesus knew that deep down in his heart Peter desired to follow him, even though Peter's understanding and capabilities were dramatically limited. Jesus knew Peter well enough to call him the rock upon which he would build his church (Matthew 16:18); yet Jesus also knew Peter well enough to predict accurately that before the rooster crowed twice, Peter would deny three times that he even knew Jesus at all (Mark 14:26-31).

We are like Peter: We too are truly human, with all of the frailties and limitations that brings. And just as he understood Peter, Jesus also understands us. Jesus knows that there are times when we want to follow, yet there are other times when we choose to shy away. But Jesus' call to Peter was to follow, not at a distance—not in the shadows, afraid of what might happen next—but to move into the light and follow boldly, whatever may come our way. This is Jesus' call to us as well. Jesus knows how limited our resources are. He knows that life is full of choices, temptations, complex situations where we become confused and frightened. Yet he calls us to follow him anyway, closely and not at a distance.

We are entering into the season of Lent, the season that marks a recommitment to discipline and focus as we follow Jesus. Each year, Lent is an opportunity to choose, again and again, how we will follow—whether it will be in the shadows or in the light, at a distance or by Jesus' side. Like the people who greeted Jesus as he entered Jerusalem for his final week on earth, we have the opportunity during this unique time to choose how close we will get to him. Remember, the authorities and the public watched his every move. Will we hang in there with him? Will we be loud about our hosannas, or will we wait and watch? Will we wave our palm branches with gusto, or will we simply hold them uneasily? Will we go with Jesus to the garden? Will we stay awake with him while he prays and wrestles with the terror of his impending future? Or, like one who betrayed him, will we choose to sell him out for money—and if so, how much will we take? How close to the fire will we get as we stand in the courtyard?

Living the Jesus way is never easy. It wasn't easy for Peter, and it isn't easy for us. While surface religious activity seems acceptable, even easy, we live in a time when the culture around us is often unreceptive to those who take their faith beyond the confines of their houses of worship. Jesus understands our difficulty. He warned us about it when he described what it takes to be his follower—putting aside selfish ambition and shouldering our cross (Matthew 16:24). Jesus invites us to follow, not at a distance but by his side. He carries his cross, and we carry ours.

For many of us, Jesus' words about shouldering our cross have come to represent the bad things in our lives. We see those bad things that we feel to be unique to our lives as the crosses that we have to bear. To be sure, there is an element of truth in this concept of shouldering our cross. Jesus does not desire that we run from suffering. We must deal with it head on and look to God for strength as we persevere.

That truth, however, is only part of what Jesus means when he tells us that to be his followers we have to shoulder our cross. A deeper meaning lies in *how* we follow. We are to follow in the same way that Jesus leads. We abandon selfish ambition in favor of service in the Jesus way. As Jesus gave of himself, we give of ourselves. We reach out to others just as he reached out to others. As Jesus loved, so do we love. As Jesus sacrificed himself for us, so do we sacrifice ourselves for others. We follow by picking up the cross. Jesus' cross becomes our cross; his love becomes our love; his sacrifice becomes our sacrifice.

Following as Jesus leads is difficult. It is difficult because there is no such thing as an easy Jesus. The theatrical release of Mel Gibson's film *The Passion of the Christ* was a rare event, capturing the attention of religious and secular media alike. The film's graphic depiction of the brutal torture Jesus endured through the Crucifixion, along with the nature of the personal sacrifice that entailed, caused many people to deeply search their soul and confront their preconceived ideas about Jesus. In an op-ed piece printed in the *Los Angeles Times*, one commentator had this to say:

> The biggest problem I have with *The Passion* . . . isn't the violence. It is with the protagonist. The guy on the screen is nothing like that insipid, tunic-wearing, lamb-carrying, two-dimensional, felt-faced Jesus from Sunday school. That Jesus was easy. He could be molded and crafted like Play-Doh into anything I—or anyone else—wanted from him. ("Gimme That New-Time Religion—a Play-Doh Jesus," by David Kuo; *Los Angeles Times*, March 8, 2004; page B11)

Following the real Jesus—not our own personal, moldable version—requires a radical lifestyle. It can't be done at a distance. It does not guarantee convenience or comfort. In fact, if you're following the Jesus way, chances are you're going to be very uncomfortable, because the Jesus who shouldered his cross isn't "moldable, pliable, malleable—not even huggable. He's determined. He knows who he is and why he's doing what he's doing" ("Gimme That New-Time Religion—a Play-Doh Jesus," *Los Angeles Times*). If you are going to follow *beside* Jesus, rather than at a distance, you have to be right in the thick of things, close to the fire where everyone can see exactly who you are.

Wendy Murray Zoba wrote about an experience she had with her sons in the wake of the Columbine school-shooting tragedy. Her seventeen-year-old son had just come home from a youth group gathering and said, "When I die, I want you to play the Supertones' 'Heaven' at my memorial service." Zoba says that her heart skipped a few beats before she agreed. She described her thoughts:

> My son and I brought different assumptions to that moment. My assumption was: Parents are not supposed to bury their children. His assumption was: To serve the Lord means you think about your memorial service. This was a post-Columbine conversation. ("Elegy for a Jesus Freak," by Wendy Murray Zoba; *Christianity Today*, December 6, 1999, Vol. 43, No. 14; page 70)

Zoba's two sons had been reading the book *Jesus Freaks*, by the Christian rock group dcTalk in collaboration with The Voice of the Martyrs. *Jesus Freaks* is a book written for teenagers that highlights martyrdoms of people all over the world, from the disciple Stephen to

Cassie Bernall, one of the students who died in the Columbine shooting. The testimony of a young Russian named Ivan, who in 1970 served in the Soviet military at the age of eighteen, particularly struck Zoba's son Jon. In an attempt to make him renounce his Christianity, Ivan was forced to stand in subzero temperatures wearing his summer uniform for twelve nights. Yet, this was Ivan's response: "A lark threatened with death for singing would still continue to sing. She cannot renounce her nature. Neither can we Christians." ("Elegy for a Jesus Freak," *Christianity Today*)

It's probably safe to speculate that the majority of us who are reading this book right now don't feel in danger of being tortured for our beliefs. But if there is no physical danger, then why is it so hard for us to follow Jesus? Why do we follow at such a distance? Why do we lurk anonymously in the shadows, away from the light of the fire?

I believe the answer is deceptively simple. It *is* risky business to follow Jesus; however, if we aren't in danger of being killed for our belief, that safety provides us with a false sense of security, a feeling that following in the Jesus way is really not that difficult. In addition to our sense of security, we have recreated the Jesus we have chosen to follow, abandoning the determined Messiah who proclaimed himself to be "the way, the truth, and the life" (see John 14:6). Instead, we have co-opted him for our own purposes—*my* way, *my* truth, *my* life. We mold this pliable Jesus in order to validate our personal successes and our views on political and social issues. Some of us would say "our" Jesus supports faith-based charities and is against gay marriage. Others of us would say "our" Jesus is against all war except the "war on poverty" and favors gun control. "Our" Jesus might stand politically either on the left or on the right; it all depends on who is doing the following. The sad truth is that many of us are not doing the following at all; we are merely bringing Jesus along on our journey.

This false sense of security and our creation of a "Jesus in our own image" hinder us from recognizing the radical nature of the Jesus way. Jesus' words to take up our cross become a faint echo heard only on Sundays and drowned out by the clamor of our lives during the rest of the week. The concept that Jesus may have taken the lashes of hell for a reason that had nothing to do with productivity or profit, success or appearance, diminishes in the face of images from Madison Avenue. The idea that he actually meant what he said about caring for the poor—that he was serious when he said that loving him requires it—becomes foreign (Matthew 19:16-23; 25:31-46). Our memory of Jesus' words about wealth fades so much that we forget how hard it is for the rich to enter the kingdom of heaven (Matthew 19:16-23) and what a bad idea it is to profiteer in Jesus' Father's house (John 2:13-16). We follow but at a distance, never getting close enough to the fire to feel its heat, never leaving the shadows long enough to be transformed.

Regardless of what we have made it, the Jesus way is truly risky business. As Wendy Murray Zoba discovered in talking to her sons, our young people possibly understand the extreme nature of following Jesus better than we do. They realize that in a culture inundated by extremes—extreme sports, extreme makeovers—Christians need to be as potent as the culture in which we find ourselves, and that can't be done at a distance. It requires getting close enough to the fire to feel the intensity of its heat. In the words of dcTalk, it's about not caring whether others label us Jesus freaks, " 'cause there ain't no disguising the truth." ("Elegy for a Jesus Freak," *Christianity Today*)

Following Jesus is not about co-opting him for our own purposes. It's about being open to the radical nature of Jesus' life, death, and resurrection. David Kuo's description of *The Passion of the Christ* is appropriate for our understanding:

> *The Passion* is so hard because it presents Jesus as we've never seen him and reveals a truth: Come face to face with Jesus in any way and prepare to squirm, or maybe even to hate him. He arouses that kind of passion and should make all of us who use his name for anything be very, very careful. ("Gimme That New-Time Religion—a Play-Doh Jesus," *Los Angeles Times*)

Following in the Jesus way is about coming face to face with Jesus, following as he leads, risking rejection from people who disagree. It requires that we reach out in love to people who aren't always the easiest to love, or to those whom others have deemed to be unworthy of our love. It's about opening our hearts to the possibility of pain and hurt when others refuse to love us in return. Following means moving out of the shadows and into the light of the fire close enough to feel its heat, close enough maybe even to get burned. The Jesus way is risky because it's all about relationships—our relationship with God and our relationships with others on God's behalf. Carrying our cross alongside Jesus requires that we make ourselves vulnerable in order that Christ might be seen through us, and that Christ's love might be reflected in our lives. It requires that we solidly stand against injustice and in solidarity with all who are oppressed in order that others can taste God's justice and mercy.

In the movie *Now and Then*, four women who shared a life-shaping summer as young girls reunite after twenty years. As they reminisce about that unforgettable summer, Demi Moore's character, Sam, reflects on her attempts to protect herself from pain, saying, "If you don't fall in love, you can't get hurt." Her friend Roberta (Rosie O'Donnell) replies, "Yeah, but it sure is lonely all by yourself." Continuing, Sam considers the idea that rather than shielding herself from hurt, she has insulated herself from fulfillment. She finally declares, "I've been so afraid of the bad things that I've missed out on the good."

Our spiritual lives can be much like Sam's experience. If we avoid the risk of living close to the fire, if we follow at a distance playing it safe, we insulate ourselves from the power God offers us when we immerse ourselves in the Jesus way. We may avoid the difficulty and challenge, but we will also miss the deep meaning and significance. Yet, when we determine to follow Jesus side by side, shouldering our cross as he shouldered his, the spirit of Jesus permeates our entire being. It is this spirit of the one who was strong enough to offer himself at Calvary for us that dwells within us. His strength becomes our strength, his boldness becomes our boldness, his courage becomes our courage.

In 1986, Boston Red Sox pitcher Roger Clemens played in his first All-Star game. He hadn't hit in years because of the American League's designated hitter rule, so when he came up to bat in the second inning, he was very nervous. Clemens took a few practice swings and got into his stance. New York Mets pitcher Dwight Gooden, who had won the Cy Young award the previous year, wound up and threw a fastball that zoomed right by Clemens. With an embarrassed smile, Clemens stepped out of the batter's box, turned to catcher Cary Carter, and asked, "Is that what my pitches look like?" Carter replied, "You bet!" Clemens returned to the batter's box, only to be unceremoniously struck out by Gooden. He went on, however, to pitch three perfect innings and be named the game's MVP.

Roger Clemens got a fresh reminder of how overpowering a good fastball is, and he pitched with far greater boldness from then on. If we never take the risk and move closer to where the action is, if we never risk abandoning the Jesus we have created in our image in favor of the real thing, we will never fully understand the depth of the strength, courage, and boldness available to us in our walk of faith; we will never understand how overpowering a good fastball really is.

Several years ago on Good Friday, we closed our worship service with these words:

> I choose to follow Christ's path. I won't give up, shut up, let up until I have stayed up, stored up, prayed up for the cause of Christ. I am a disciple of Jesus. I must go until he comes, give until I drop, preach until I know, and work until he stops me. And when he comes for his own, he will have no problem recognizing me. I belong to him. (*Handbook for Multi-Sensory Worship*, page 44)

That's following. That's what Jesus meant when he told us we need to shoulder our cross. That's what it means to walk beside Jesus while he carries his. But that kind of following requires moving close to the fire. If we don't do that—if we keep our distance and remain in the shadows—we will never truly experience the power of Jesus in our lives, and we will never live in the abundant way that Jesus promises.

Study / Discussion Questions

1. Reflect on your motivations for entering into this study. What kind of choices are you facing as you seek to follow Jesus? What hurdles have you encountered recently? What confirmations have you received that you are on the right track? (If it would be helpful to you, make some notes about your experience.)

2. Read again the author's description of the apostle Peter in the first few paragraphs of the chapter. How does this description resonate with your experience of following Jesus?

3. How have you interpreted Jesus' words that we must shoulder our cross and follow him (see Luke 9:23)? Share or write a brief description of the crosses you feel you are bearing.

4. Spend some time prayerfully considering the additional meaning of shouldering the cross as related to *how* we follow: Jesus' cross becomes our cross, his love our love, his sacrifice our sacrifice. What might change in your life if you entertained this additional meaning?

5. The author says that oftentimes, we are guilty of bringing Jesus

along on our journey rather than following Jesus on his. How might this be true for you? Make an honest assessment of the ways in which you might be using Jesus to validate your personal successes or goals, or your personal views (for example, on social or political issues).

6. What risks are you willing to take to follow Jesus more closely? What commitments (or recommitments) do you need to make in order to move closer to the fire?

Focus for the Coming Week

Recall these words:

I choose to follow Christ's path. I won't give up, shut up, let up until I have stayed up, stored up, prayed up for the cause of Christ. I am a disciple of Jesus. I must go until he comes, give until I drop, preach until I know, and work until he stops me. And when he comes for his own, he will have no problem recognizing me. I belong to him. (*Handbook for Multi-Sensory Worship*, page 44)

Spend some time in prayer this week focusing on your choices and commitments in following Jesus. Allow the Holy Spirit to enliven your heart, empowering you and providing you with a sense of boldness to follow in Jesus' way.

Prayer

Lord Jesus, please forgive me for following you at a distance. Empower me to shoulder my cross and walk by your side. Fill me with boldness to risk moving out of the shadows and into the light— the heat—of the fire, to choose on this day to live in such a way that you will have no problem recognizing me. Amen.

Jesus, in Real Time

Oh, there is so much more I want to tell you, but you can't bear it now. When the Spirit of truth comes, he will guide you into all truth. He will not be presenting his own ideas; he will be telling you what he has heard. He will tell you about the future. He will bring me glory by revealing to you whatever he receives from me.
John 16:12-14 (NLT)

We began our journey together last week by focusing on our tendency to be like Peter, avoiding the fire as we follow Jesus, remaining in the shadows, following at a distance. I mentioned that one of the reasons for our difficulty in following as Jesus leads is that we have co-opted Jesus for our own purposes, inviting him along on our journey rather than following him on his. Creating Jesus in our own image is an easy thing to do because for many of us Jesus isn't *real*; Jesus is simply a two-dimensional caricature like those we have seen placed on felt boards to illustrate Bible stories—flat, lifeless, old-fashioned. We are tempted to recreate Jesus because Jesus is imprisoned in our memories, no longer an alive, vibrant part of our experience.

Some would say that the church hasn't helped us with this temptation, that in fact the church is often the very source of Jesus' chains, having forged link after link of tradition to hold him. Many of us are confident we know Jesus because we know all the Bible stories about him, we have studied him, we're familiar with what he did and said two thousand years ago. Because we know the Bible, we know what he said to the woman at the well. We know that he healed the blindness of Bartimaeus. We know that when he healed ten lepers, only one of those men came back to thank him. We know

22

enough about Jesus to have trapped him, to have painted him as a still life: Here he is blessing the children; here he is visiting with Mary and Martha; here he is frozen in time by the stories we know so well.

There were other folks who knew their Bible well too. They knew the stories of their faith. They knew the laws that governed their relationship with God. These folks brought a woman to Jesus. She had been caught in the act of adultery. I've always thought it interesting that she was the only one brought before Jesus; after all, I've never known of anyone who physically committed adultery by themselves. Regardless, she was the only one who was brought before Jesus by these people who knew their Bible so well. They knew that according to the Bible she should be executed for her sin, and they wanted to know what Jesus thought should be done (John 8:1-11). Jesus' reaction tells me that while these people knew their Bible, they didn't know *him*. Because after thinking quietly for a bit, doodling in the sand with a stick, Jesus challenged the one among them who was without sin to throw the first stone at the accused woman. Stunned, all in the crowd dropped their rocks and left.

On a later occasion, when two of Jesus' disciples were walking to Emmaus, still reeling from the horror of Jesus' crucifixion, he made himself present to them; but they were unable to recognize him (Luke 24:13-16). What they knew was the *past*—Jesus had been killed—yet he was walking right beside them *in the present,* and they didn't even realize it.

We are like those two disciples: So much has happened to us, so much history has passed, that we are unable to recognize Jesus walking beside us in real time. We're like the folks who knew their Bible so well that they had already picked up their rocks. Instead of experiencing Jesus' presence, instead of hearing him afresh in our current circumstances, instead of tapping into the power that Jesus offers us right now, we've chained him to the past, draining him of his power for our lives right now and making him completely unrecognizable to us.

It's dangerous to live your life with a past focus, with a two-dimensional felt-board Jesus. It's dangerous because we end up following a tradition, or even the Bible, instead of following *Jesus,* God's living Word. We have no recognition of Jesus in real time, his *real* presence, his "right now" presence, so we follow at a distance created by the chains of the past.

But that is not what Jesus promised us. Jesus never said: "I'm going to give myself up to be crucified. I'm going to willingly die an incredibly painful and degrading death, so that you will be able to remember me with cute Sunday school pictures and out-of-focus paintings." What Jesus *did* promise is a never-ending presence—his Spirit, his power. He promised to provide us with a means for guidance, direction, and power, not just now but into the future to the end of the ages. Jesus said, "When the Spirit of truth comes, he will guide you into all truth. He will not be presenting his own ideas; he will be telling you what he has heard. He will tell you about the future" (John 16:13, NLT).

As a Sunday school teacher tried to explain that Jesus is always with us even though we can't see him, a four-year-old piped up, "I already know that. He's the one who opens the door when we go into a store!" While Jesus may not be in charge of grocery-store doors, we seem to have forgotten that he has the power to be real in our lives *right now* and the power to be active in our lives far into the future. We seem to have forgotten what it means to be in relationship with a *living* God, a God in the present tense, a God who is with us *in real time*. If we are to follow in the Jesus way, side-by-side as Jesus leads, we must recognize that Jesus offers more than sentimental memories and demands more of us as well. He offers power for our lives and our world and demands that we follow in ways that allow his power to flow through us. Jesus in real time is the only Jesus we can truly know. We can know *about* the Jesus who walked this earth two thousand years ago, but we can only truly know Jesus in real time through the power of the Holy Spirit. This is the Jesus we are called to follow side-by-side rather than at a distance, opening ourselves to his direction for our present and our future.

When we open ourselves to the possibility of knowing Jesus in real time, we are able to experience power as did Ananias, a disciple who lived in Damascus. God spoke to Ananias in a vision and told him to go to a house on Straight Street; when he got there, he would find a man named Saul, whom God had also given a vision of a man named Ananias restoring his sight (Acts 9:10-12). Now, Ananias was not enthusiastic about following these instructions, because they put him right in the thick of things. Following Jesus in real time, up close and personal, would mean finding this Saul and coming face to face with the one who had been arresting and persecuting Christians with unbelievable zeal and determination. What Ananias knew about the past made him nervous about this kind of future. Despite his nervousness, Ananias obeyed. He followed, trusting the real presence of Jesus to direct him into the future. When Ananias arrived at the house, he found Saul, laid his hands on him, and said, "Brother Saul, the Lord Jesus, who appeared to you on the road, has sent me so that you may get your sight back and be filled with the Holy Spirit" (Acts 9:17, NLT). Acts 9 tells us that "instantly something like scales fell from Saul's eyes, and he regained his sight" (verse 18, NLT).

Ananias could not have discovered how to follow Jesus in that particular moment simply by reading his Bible. Even if he had known Jesus personally, he couldn't have known how to follow Jesus in this particular situation. Ananias had to experience the presence of Jesus in real time in order to be guided into the future, in order to follow in the way that Jesus desired.

Our present-tense Jesus, the Jesus in real time, is not in the same form as he was two thousand years ago. The beard is gone; no more sandals. That's why we don't recognize him. That's why the disciples walking to Emmaus didn't recognize him. We're able to follow Jesus closely, side by side, when we live in the presence of the Holy Spirit. It's the power of the Holy Spirit that makes Jesus present to us now. It's Holy Spirit power that channels everything to us that Jesus desires us to know. It's the Spirit that guides us into the future, outlining for us exactly how we are to follow.

The disciples may have had the privilege of living in the presence of Jesus; but we have the privilege of having the presence of Jesus living in us. This is what Paul was desperate for us to understand when he said, "For this is the secret: Christ lives in you, and this is your assurance that you will share in his glory" (Colossians 1:27, NLT). Each of us is a temple of the Holy Spirit. The problem for us as we follow Jesus is that we are looking "out there"—beyond us—when Jesus in real time, through the Spirit, is right here within us.

Great spiritual power is available to us when we allow the Holy Spirit to make Jesus real to us. A few years back a provocative illustration of what can happen when we follow Jesus in real time came from a very unlikely source. The musical artist Madonna released a video for her song "Like a Prayer," which points to the power of experiencing Jesus in real time. In Madonna's typically controversial style, "Like a Prayer" challenges our assumptions on many fronts—our assumptions about the relationship of the church to the world, about racial relations, about the sensual aspects of spirituality. Regardless of your view of Madonna, it is impossible to watch this video without being moved to spiritual reflection.

Like many music videos, "Like a Prayer" is not simply a visual production of Madonna singing her song; rather, it's a mini-drama accompanied throughout by the words and music of the song. It opens with a twilight scene; Madonna is running as though trying to escape something. She stumbles and falls as two quick images flash, that of a burning cross and that of men violently attacking a woman. As all this unfolds, Madonna begins to sing about life as mystery, and how we all must stand alone. Looking up from the ground, she sees a church, its windows glowing invitingly. The camera focuses on the church as she continues to sing about hearing her name called, and how that experience has a feeling like home. Madonna enters the church, and it is clear that this is a place of comfort, refuge, and safety. Candles provide a warm and peaceful glow. As the song begins in earnest, Madonna is drawn deeper into the church toward a statue of a black man behind an altar gate. She looks with wonder at the statue some believe represents Jesus, but most agree is a statue depicting Martin de Porres, an Afro-Peruvian saint. Interestingly, Martin was a lay brother of the Dominican order who carried out his ministry in Peru on behalf of the sick, the poor, and African slaves. Pope John XXIII canonized de Porres in 1962; and Martin, the child of a Spanish father and a free black woman from Lima, has become known as the patron saint of interracial justice. This is significant background information given the emphasis on interracial relations that so clearly undergirds Madonna's video.

Mysteriously, tears form in the statue's eyes as Madonna kneels before it. She appears to be singing directly to the statue. She sings that she hears his voice, and it sounds like the sighing of an angel, leaving her with no choice but to follow. She kisses the statue's feet, then stands, opens the gate, and lovingly touches its cheek. Suddenly the statue comes to life. Madonna's vocals describe the experience of a child having an adult whisper to her, as the now-living man whispers in her ear, kisses her on the forehead, and leaves the church. Madonna looks down and sees a knife, which she picks up, and then accidentally cuts herself. When the camera reveals her hands, we see that Madonna has received the stigmata, the wounds of Christ, on her own hands.

The video continues with an African American church choir joining Madonna in singing. As they sing, many quick images unfold. Having recognized the stigmata on her hands, Madonna leaves the church. She witnesses a group of white men attacking a white woman, and she makes eye contact with the leader of the gang as they run away. The statue-come-to-life, now a black man, also witnesses the violence and rushes to the woman's aid as police cars arrive. The police assume this man is the perpetrator and arrest him, while the real criminal smirks at Madonna in the shadows. All of these images are interspersed with the choir singing energetically.

Significantly, the musical zenith occurs at this point, and Madonna sings while dancing in front of large burning crosses. Her words refer again to life as mystery and how each person must stand alone. She sings of feeling at home at the sound of her name being called. As the bridge continues, the scene shifts back to the church, and Madonna and the choir sing and dance joyfully. While Madonna may or may not agree, it is as though she is singing about Jesus. His voice is like a prayer, like music. His voice is a mystery; it's like a dream, and he is not what he seems. Jesus' voice is like a prayer, and she has no choice when she hears it. Again, quick images dart before us as we watch—the statue's tears, Madonna and the black man kissing, the burning crosses. The statue-come-to-life returns to his place behind the gate; and as the camera holds on his face, it transforms into the face of the arrested black man behind the bars of a jail cell. As the song fades, the camera pulls back to reveal Madonna speaking to the policeman. The officer takes his keys and unlocks the cell door as a curtain drops and the video ends.

In a short span of time, Madonna has given us quite a lot to think about. I don't know Madonna's motivation. I don't know any personal details about her faith or what her exact intentions were in making this video. However, I do know that God uses many vehicles in order to touch us and reveal truth to us. Madonna's theology may not be completely accurate, and her use of sexuality may be controversial; but in "Like a Prayer," she has touched upon a great truth that is crucial for us as we seek to follow in the Jesus way.

When Madonna sings about the experience of hearing her name called and feeling at home, there is a connection to the experience of following Jesus in real time. Following in the Jesus way is about hearing our names called. It is about feeling at home with God. Unfortunately, we often don't hear our names or feel at home; instead it's all stiff statues and empty symbols. Yet following is about returning to the joy of belonging that fills us up so much that we can't help but dance. That's what Jesus in the present tense is all about. And Madonna's video illustrates more. In her own way, Madonna points to the fact that following in the Jesus way is not a private matter. It doesn't happen exclusively within the walls of the church; in fact, inside the walls is not where it happens at all. It happens in the hearts of people. It happens in the world.

When we experience Jesus in real time, barriers are broken down, gates are opened, relationships are mended, bridges are built. When we allow the power of Jesus to escape the confines of plaster statues and felt-board pictures, to actually touch us in the present and lead us into the future, lives are changed. It's significant that it is Madonna's expression of love that brings the statue of Saint Martin to life. Madonna herself becomes a force of liberation, as was Saint Martin. Saint Martin, freed from life behind the gate, leaves the church and enters the world. Madonna, having found herself marked like Christ, moves out into the world as well.

As Christ followers, we too are marked; and Jesus calls us to follow him into the world. The test of our faith is not how it is contained within the church; it's not about our sweet memories of a cutout Jesus. The test of our faith is whether it can guide our experience in the world, in the here and now. Our faith is not in a two-dimensional Jesus, a cartoon picture stuck on a felt board in our memories. Our faith is in the real Jesus, who lives in the real world, our world, through the power of the Holy Spirit. We follow the one who has the power to set us free, to deepen our lives, to heal our wounds, to mend our relationships, to break down the walls that separate us and tear down the barriers that hinder us from loving each other. This is Jesus in real time; the Jesus who wants to be alive within you.

The apostle Paul prayed for his churches constantly, asking God to "give [them] spiritual wisdom and understanding, so that [they] might grow in [their] knowledge of God" (Ephesians 1:17, NLT). That is my prayer for you as you continue this Lenten journey: "I pray that your hearts will be flooded with light so that you can understand the wonderful future he has promised to those he called. I want you to realize what a rich and glorious inheritance he has given to his people.

I pray that you will begin to understand the incredible greatness of his power for us who believe him" (Ephesians 1:18-19a, NLT). That light is the light of Christ, the light of Jesus in real time, who has promised you a wonderful future—a rich and glorious inheritance. That light is the light of Jesus, the Jesus who provides incredible greatness of power to all who believe him—the power to love, the power to heal, the power to reach out. May you make that light your own; may you make that power your own.

Study / Discussion Questions

1. Reflect on and discuss the difference between knowing Jesus and knowing *about* Jesus. How has that difference played itself out in your life? Has your experience of Jesus been of the more two-dimensional variety; or have you experienced a living, dynamic Jesus "in real time"? (If it is helpful, make notes to gain clarity on your experience.)

2. The author describes the story in Acts 9 of Ananias communicating with the Lord. Read Acts 9:10-17 and reflect on or discuss: When or how have you experienced Jesus communicating with you in real time? What are the benefits of such communication? In your opinion, what effect would it have upon our ability to receive Jesus' message if we focused solely upon the Bible or tradition?

3. In describing Madonna's video for "Like a Prayer," the author said that following Jesus in real time is about hearing our names called; it is about feeling at home with God. Has this been your experience? Why or why not? As you are comfortable doing so, share your thoughts in explaining your answer.

4. In your own life, what gates need to be opened? What barriers need to be brought down? What relationships need to be mended? What bridges need to be built?

5. At the close of the chapter, the author said that the test of our faith is whether it can guide our experience in the world—in the here and now. What might need to change in your life in order for you to be more receptive and responsive to the guidance of faith?

Focus for the Coming Week

We follow the one who has the power to set us free, to deepen our lives, to heal our wounds, to mend our relationships, to break down

the walls that separate us and tear down the barriers that hinder us from loving each other. This is Jesus in real time, the Jesus who wants to be alive within you. Claim that power for yourself this week.

Prayer

Forgive me, Lord Jesus, for following my two-dimensional, flat image of you rather than experiencing your presence in real time. Please help me to hear you calling my name so that I might feel at home in you. Use me as a channel of your power to break down barriers, open gates, mend relationships, and build bridges. Keep me following in real time so that I feel your presence alive within me. Amen.

Little Pentecosts

The person who trusts me will not only do what I'm doing
but even greater things. . . . You can count on it.
                    John 14:12 (THE MESSAGE)

I can do everything with the help of Christ who gives me
the strength I need.
                    Philippians 4:13 (NLT)

Last week, we looked at our need to experience Jesus in real time in order to follow with power and integrity; we need to release Jesus from the chains of the past in order that his Spirit might operate in new and dynamic ways in the present and into the future. At the heart of that need is the fact that we serve a mighty God. Following in the Jesus way entails recognizing that it is an awesome God who empowers us; and as we experience Jesus in real time, we are given the courage to follow closely and are empowered to do great things. In fact, Jesus promised that when we are in touch with him in real time, we will have the power to do greater things even than he did.

Scripture attests to the validity of Jesus' promise. While crowds of people followed Jesus during his earthly ministry in Judea, the spirit of Jesus worked through the disciples to give birth to a body of believers that has been growing ever since as the fire of the Holy Spirit spread to the ends of the earth. Once again, Peter and the other disciples provide a significant model for us. While Jesus was on earth, they were followers, students. They didn't always understand the message or the methods of Jesus' ministry, and they certainly were not able to perform even a single miracle in Jesus' presence. Their failures and weaknesses were most apparent. In fact, Judas betrayed Jesus and

31

then killed himself in despair; and when the pressure was on, Peter denied he ever knew Jesus. Finally, in the wake of the Crucifixion, everyone took refuge behind locked doors, hiding in terror, expecting reprisal. Yet these terrified followers didn't remain students, and they didn't remain terrified. Instead, they were transformed. They were empowered by the Holy Spirit to be more than simply followers of Jesus; no longer students, they became messengers of the gospel. This transformation didn't take place because of the bodily presence of the Jesus they had followed those many months; it didn't happen because of his teaching or through the witness of his miracles and healings. The disciples were transformed into messengers by the presence of Jesus in real time, through the power of the Holy Spirit.

We call the event of the disciples' transformation *Pentecost,* that miraculous event that took place fifty days after Easter and launched the spread of the gospel throughout the world. What we don't always realize is that the Holy Spirit has been responsible for a myriad of little Pentecosts ever since. A pivotal event in my own life, about which I have shared in other contexts and writings, occurred in 1996 when I had been in ministry only a short while. Due to the young age of my children, I had been appointed part-time to a local church as an associate; and while my work was focused mainly in the important areas of children's worship and teaching, I had very little responsibility overall. Then I was invited to attend an evangelism conference, the Order of the Flame. With its emphasis on evangelism, the focus of the entire conference was on reaching others for Christ. It was a powerful time, and I was surrounded by many talented people who were doing exciting things for God's kingdom. The last event of the conference was a worship service. There was dynamic music, great preaching. It was an awesome worship experience. We closed our time with prayer. Everyone stood, and people spontaneously offered their prayers aloud.

As the praying became more intense, I suddenly felt the powerful presence of God's Holy Spirit—not just in the service itself but within *me.* As I continued to listen to the prayers being lifted, I was overwhelmed by the spiritual depth that surrounded me, feeling out of my league. It didn't seem possible that I could do the types of ministry these folks were doing with such power. I began to feel intensely unworthy, ill-equipped to do whatever it was God was calling me to do. In that moment, I was ready to bolt out of the room. It was truly a crisis, not necessarily of faith but of calling.

As I began to follow my instincts and leave as quickly as possible, I felt the full weight of God's power upon me. I couldn't even move. I wanted to run, but I couldn't move. I sat down, convinced there was no way I could do what God was calling me to do. Then suddenly I heard the voice of Jesus within me, saying, "You *are* ill-equipped; you *don't* have all the ability. But that doesn't matter; because I am *not* ill-equipped. You can do this—you *will* do this, because *I* am your source of power; and it is I who will work through you."

God moments; "little Pentecosts"; times when we experience Jesus in real time. From that time on, everything changes—who we are, how we live. These aren't events that exist only in the stories of our faith. They happen every day to believers all over the world, and following in the Jesus way requires that we be open to those life-changing, faith-shaping little Pentecosts.

Being open to experiencing our own little Pentecosts is about recognizing that each of us has a life mission. It's that purpose for which God created you, for which God has placed unique gifts and talents and passions within you. Often, you can trace your "God mission" back to some particular passion that has been in your life for a long time. Moses is a great example of connecting our passion with our God mission.

Moses had a passion: It was the racism and oppression of the Jews that he witnessed in Egypt. Even though he was a Jew, Moses had grown up in Pharaoh's court, in the environment of privilege afforded the king's family. From that vantage point, he saw the enslavement and oppression of his people and realized that it wasn't right. From that moment, Moses' passion began brewing inside him, a distinct hint that his God mission would move him beyond the arena of being Pharaoh's adopted son. But the events of Moses' life disconnected him from his original passion and his God mission; and he found himself in Midian, far from Egypt, tending the sheep of his father-in-law (see Exodus 2:1-22).

It can be easy to live our lives disconnected from our passion and, as a result, from our God mission. That disconnect is often one of the things that keeps us following at a distance. But following as Jesus leads requires that we connect—or reconnect—with our passion, that we then discover our God mission and act upon it. It requires that we be open to a little Pentecost—or a burning bush—in order to receive insight from God as to exactly how we are to follow.

33

The problem is that our God mission is almost always tremendously bigger than we are. That's exactly what Moses discovered. As he was tending his father-in-law's sheep, he experienced a little Pentecost. God captured Moses' attention in a miraculous way—through an encounter with a burning bush—and gave him an amazing mission: "I am sending you to Pharaoh. You will lead my people, the Israelites, out of Egypt" (Exodus 3:10, NLT).

Moses had a hard time accepting his God mission because he, like us, had limited his destiny to what he believed he could accomplish with his own strength and resources. He was no longer an Egyptian prince; he was now a simple sheepherder. In the same way that I was ready to walk out on my calling because I felt ill-equipped, Moses tried to convince God to send someone else: "Who am I to appear before Pharaoh? . . . How can you expect me to lead the Israelites out of Egypt? . . . They won't believe me! They won't do what I tell them. . . . I'm just not a good speaker. . . . Lord, please! Send someone else" (Exodus 3:11; 4:1, 10, 13, NLT).

We struggle to follow Jesus closely, in sync with our God mission, because that mission is bigger than we can imagine. We are limited by our detailed lists of past failures, our internal sense of inadequacy, the unhealthy level (whether too high or too low) of our self-esteem. All of those roadblocks shape what we perceive our life to be about. We create a picture in our minds of what we will become, and it's almost always smaller than what God intends. Back when Mark McGwire and Sammy Sosa were racing to break the Major League homerun record, the newspapers talked about McGwire's attitude before the season started. They said that before the season began, he had created a picture in his mind. McGwire knew that that was the year he would break the record, and he held the picture of it happening in his mind throughout the season.

Unfortunately, rather than picturing an unbelievable future, we often choose to place a limited picture in our mind's eye. The picture that I held in my mind when I attended the evangelism conference was limited to the way I was doing ministry at that time. I couldn't comprehend what God had in store for me because it was bigger than I could imagine and went far beyond common sense.

That's significant. As we seek to follow in the Jesus way, we need to recognize that more often than not, rather than being rooted in common sense, the Jesus way *defies* common sense. I discussed this idea in *Knowing God: Making God the Main Thing in My Life* (a volume in the Sisters: Bible Study for Women series) when I highlighted the story of Jesus' friends, Mary, Martha, and Lazarus. Lazarus was sick, very near death, and his two sisters, Mary and Martha, sent for Jesus. For whatever reason, Jesus was delayed; and by the time he arrived, Lazarus had already been dead for several days. Of course, this fact didn't faze Jesus, and he immediately instructed them to open the tomb. Martha, on the other hand, was limited by common sense. The picture she had in her mind was of a body that had been dead for days. "We can't open the tomb! Ugh! The stench!"

How many times have we limited ourselves to the pictures created by common sense? *I could never do that; I'm too old; My children are too young; I don't have the right degree.* We are like Martha. But Jesus shakes his head and says, "Didn't I tell you that you will see God's glory if you believe?" (John 11:40, NLT); and Lazarus walks out of the tomb alive!

We follow an awesome God! A God who can do great things, even with limited resources. This means that our life mission isn't about what we can imagine about ourselves. It is about what God imagines about us. When we imagine ourselves, our response to the mission God sets before us is often: *That's impossible! I'm not smart enough! I've been divorced! I'm in recovery! I'm this. . . . I'm that. . . . I'm not this. . . . I'm not that!* But God says that none of that matters. None of that matters because our life mission isn't about what we can do for God. Our life mission is what God is going to do through us.

Remember Moses? "Who am I to appear before Pharaoh?" (Exodus 3:11, NLT). God says, "It's not about what you can imagine about yourself. It's what I imagine about you." God says, "I will be with you" (verse 12). God says, "It's not about what you can do for me; it's what I am going to do through you." That revelation was at the heart of Moses' burning-bush experience, and it was at the heart of my "little Pentecost" at the conference. I was transformed when I realized that it wasn't what I was going to do for God, but what God was going to do through me.

We follow an awesome God; and when we choose to follow side by side, rather than at a distance, we experience God's power to take the ordinary and make it extraordinary. That's what happened to Moses and to the disciples, and that's what happens to us. Moses tells God that he can't speak well, that he gets tongue-tied, that he stutters (see Exodus 4:10). What is God's response? "Who makes mouths? I will be your mouth. I will give the words" (Exodus 4:11, NLT, paraphrased). Similarly Peter, who before Pentecost barely knew what to say or when to say it, is empowered to speak eloquently to the crowds all over Jerusalem (see Acts 2:1-42).

God takes the ordinary and makes it extraordinary. God puts words in our mouths and transforms the ordinary elements of our lives into powerful tools. God uses the ordinary things, all those things we don't recognize as significant, to do extraordinary things. Moses' biggest weapon, the source of extraordinary signs and miracles as he argued with Pharaoh to free God's people, was an ordinary shepherd's staff. Moses went up against Pharaoh, ruler of the most powerful kingdom on earth at that time, armed with the stick he had used for forty years herding his father-in-law's sheep.

When I was little, I spent many Sunday mornings sitting in church, bored out of my mind. I became an expert doodler. As an adult, I have many non-Christian friends; I seem to be drawn to them. I don't believe these ordinary aspects of my life are accidents. My passion is reaching out to non-Christian folks. My passion is creating worship experiences that people find relevant rather than boring. God takes the ordinary within our lives and uses it for God's purpose, often in extraordinary ways. The reality of following in the Jesus way doesn't consist of what you can do for God. It consists of recognizing what God can do through you. Thus the question we must ask ourselves is not what can I give God, but what is God doing? How can I be a part of what God is doing?

Mine is a soccer family. At one time or another, all five of us have played on various teams at various levels. My husband and two of our three children continue to play, and we all love to watch. It's particularly funny to watch little children play. When little kids play soccer, they all cluster around the ball. We call it "amoeba soccer." It's a huge crowd of kids—no positions—just a huge crowd that moves, almost as one organism, wherever the ball goes. That is what the church is supposed to be. That is what it looks like to follow Jesus side by side instead of at a distance. Christ followers look around to see what God is doing, and then they get involved; they move wherever it is that God moves.

Jesus warned that we need to walk in the light while we are able, while that light is with us, so that we won't stumble when darkness comes (see John 12:35). When we follow Jesus side by side, we don't wait until we have everything figured out. We don't wait until our life picture has been filled in with every detail. We act on what we know and trust that God's picture is infinitely greater than our own. We act on the glimpses we receive of the light of God's truth, trusting that God is working through us. Following in the Jesus way is to walk in the light before darkness arrives and the window of opportunity closes. We follow at a distance when we hear the truth of God and wait rather than walk; but the Jesus way involves action—breaking ranks, risking the radical, attempting the impossible.

Michael Slaughter, senior pastor of Ginghamsburg Church in Tipp City, Ohio, reminds us of an important truth: Miracles don't come *to* us, they come *through* us. Following Jesus, up close and in the thick of things, isn't about being all you can be or becoming the best you can be. Moses' life mission was about achieving God's purpose for God's people. Moses lived in sync with that mission not by focusing on self-fulfillment or self-actualization but by allowing God to work through him. Jesus promised that "rivers of living water will brim and spill out of the depths of anyone who believes in [him]" (John 7:37, *THE MESSAGE*). We don't follow in the Jesus way in order to achieve personal fulfillment or satisfaction, even though that may be a significant byproduct. We follow in the Jesus way in order to serve: to become a source of refreshment and healing and creativity to everyone around us.

Lent is a season of introspection, of refocusing the lens of our lives in order to gain perspective on our faith. Perspective comes when we refocus on God, who has promised to be with us, to be our mouth, to be our resource, to be our strength. Perspective comes when we refocus on God, who doesn't give miracles to us, but works miracles through us. Perspective comes when we refocus to see that following Jesus with integrity makes each of us a witness; and witnesses cannot hide in the shadows, away from the fire. Witnesses step into the light of the fire, where everyone can see. Witnesses tell the truth about what they have seen and experienced. Many of us follow at a distance because we are afraid to be a witness. We are afraid we won't be able to answer if we step close to the fire and someone recognizes us. What if they ask us about Jesus? How can we possibly answer—especially if we aren't even that sure who Jesus is? But, as we have discussed, following Jesus isn't about knowing all the details of the Jesus of the past. It's about experiencing Jesus in real time. Witnesses simply tell the truth about what they have seen and experienced. "I'm not sure who Jesus is. All I know is that he has made me different." Witnesses tell the truth about what they know, about what is happening within them right now.

Jesus said we should walk in the light while we can—not wait for some huge opportunity. Luke tells about Jesus healing a man who had been possessed by demons, legions of demons (Luke 8:26-39). Jesus had set this man free from his life of bondage, and now the man begged to be able to follow him. The man was prepared to leave his home, to follow Jesus and be a part of the amazing things Jesus was going to do. But Jesus said no to the man. He wouldn't allow him to leave his home. Instead he said, "Go back to your family and tell them all the wonderful things God has done for you" (Luke 8:39, NLT).

God desires to use you. God has placed a purpose within you, a life mission. Following Jesus is about discovering that life mission. It's guaranteed to be bigger than you can imagine, but God has surrounded you with all the tools you need to accomplish it. God also desires to work a miracle through you for another person. And, just like the ordinary tools God has provided, that person is already in your circle of influence. That is why God wants you to return home, like the man whom Jesus healed. Following Jesus is about going back to our jobs and our homes—back to our ordinary lives—and telling others about the great things God has done for us, then living in ways that show others the great things God has done for us. We may not have it all together; we may have pain or shame. But it's not how we imagine ourselves, it's how God imagines us. We walk in the light— now. We don't wait. We simply take our ordinary lives, add our experience of Jesus in real time, and allow God to create a mighty work through us.

Study / Discussion Questions

1. Reflect on your experience of the Holy Spirit. Have you experienced a "little Pentecost"—a pivotal, faith-shaping encounter with Jesus in real time?

2. What are some of your passions in life? Make a list.

3. Have you made the connection between your passions and your God mission? Reflect on or discuss the experience of making that

connection; or if this connection has not yet become clear, share your thoughts about bringing your God-given passion and mission together. It may be helpful to list some of your thoughts.

4. What are some of the things that may be hindering you from claiming your God mission, limiting you from seeing God's picture for your life? As you reflect, and prior to discussion, you may want to list these in order to get them clearly in your mind.

5. How might God be calling you to move beyond your perceived limitations, to move beyond common sense, in claiming God's purpose for your life?

Focus for the Coming Week

Commit yourself to discovering God's purpose for your life, recognizing that it is not what we can imagine about ourselves that is important but what God imagines about us. Claim God's desire to work a miracle through your life.

Prayer

Dear God, open my heart to all the little Pentecosts you wish to make manifest in my life through the example of Jesus Christ in the Holy Spirit. Please forgive me when my focus on my limitations hinders me from seeing the life mission you have created for me. Enable me to be reminded that it is not what I can imagine about myself, but it is what you imagine about me. Amen.

Kingdom People

Blessed are the poor in spirit, for theirs is the kingdom of heaven. / Blessed are those who mourn, for they will be comforted. / Blessed are the meek, for they will inherit the earth. / Blessed are those who hunger and thirst for righteousness, for they will be filled. / Blessed are the merciful, for they will receive mercy. / Blessed are the pure in heart, for they will see God. / Blessed are the peacemakers, for they will be called children of God. / Blessed are those who are persecuted for righteousness' sake, for theirs is the kingdom of heaven. / Blessed are you when people revile you and persecute you and utter all kinds of evil against you falsely on my account. / Rejoice and be glad, for your reward is great in heaven.

Matthew 5:3-12 (NRSV)

We're approaching the midway point of our time together, having used Peter's experience in the courtyard after Jesus was arrested as our metaphor for following in the Jesus way. Peter's experience raises the question of how closely we intend to follow Jesus—at a distance, away from the fire, or side by side, carrying our cross even as Jesus carries his. We've explored the importance of experiencing Jesus in real time—how releasing Jesus from the chains of the past enables us to follow him more intimately in the present reality of our lives. In conjunction with the importance of experiencing Jesus in real time is the significance of discovering God's purpose for our lives—our life mission. Opening ourselves to God's picture of our life is a crucial aspect of following Jesus side by side rather than at a distance. It is in discovering God's picture of our life that we come to a deeper understanding of *how* it is that we will follow in the context of our individual lives.

To further our understanding of what it means to intimately follow in the Jesus way, we now turn to the Beatitudes—Jesus' statements about blessedness, which can be found in Matthew 5:3-12. The Beatitudes are helpful to us because they highlight the contrast between God's kingdom and the kingdom of our world. This contrast is crucial for our understanding because following Jesus side by side places us in sharp contrast with the world around us. As Peter was recognized to be a disciple of Jesus by the light of the fire, following in the Jesus way shines the light of blessedness on us, distinguishing us from our culture and making us recognizable as Christ followers.

The first thing to notice about the Beatitudes is that Jesus didn't actually say them in the way we are used to hearing them. In the Aramaic that Jesus spoke, and the Greek in which Jesus' words were written, the verb *are* is not present in the Beatitudes; that word was used to render his words into English. Rather than statements— "Blessed are the poor in spirit"—Jesus gave us exclamations: "O the blessedness of the meek!" This is important, because the Beatitudes aren't statements about what might be, or about what could be. They are exclamations about what is. Jesus is announcing the privilege that is ours, to share with God in joy, to share the very blessedness that fills God's heart. The New Living Translation uses the action word *blesses* rather than the adjective *blessed,* which helps us understand the "is-ness"—the present tense action—of what Jesus is saying. God blesses those who hunger and thirst for righteousness! The blessedness that God offers is ours *now,* not in some future time. Jesus is announcing the present reality of God's blessing right now, in the present tense. (*The Gospel of Matthew, Vol. 1,* by William Barclay; The Westminster Press, 1975; pages 88–89).

These blessings, available right now, are quite a surprise when we consider what the world tells us affords blessing. The world would have us believe that righteous, merciful ways of living are weak. The world would have us believe that mourning leads to unhappiness. In contrast, Jesus proclaims that meekness, humility, and persecution, rather than being sources of unhappiness or misery, are actually sources of spiritual giftedness. That is the surprise of the Beatitudes—what appears to be a source of unhappiness, turns out to be a source of joy and blessedness.

The secret to the surprise of the Beatitudes can be seen in a simple explanation of the root words. We call Matthew 5:3-12 the Beatitudes because the word *beatitude*, which is Latin, simply means "blessing." The meaning of the word *blessing* comes from two sources: the Latin word *benedicere*, which means "to speak well of," and the Greek word *makarios*, which means "blessed." *Makarios* was a word used to describe the gods, and it points to a godlke joy, a kind of joy that has its secret within itself. *Makarios* is a self-contained kind of joy, a joy that does not depend on circumstance. It is independent of chance or change. These concepts combine to form our understanding of *blessing*. Unfortunately in English the idea of joy is often understood as being the same thing as "happiness." The word *blessing*—and consequently the Beatitudes themselves—has also come to be connected with a concept of happiness. The surprise comes because Jesus associates some strange things with happiness—meekness, persecution, mourning. Our surprise comes because we fall short in understanding. Our English word *happiness* contains the root *hap,* which means "chance." That root word points to the reality of human happiness—something that is more often than not dramatically affected by chance and the unfolding events of life, something that life may generate or extinguish at the blink of an eye (*The Gospel of Matthew, Vol. 1*; pages 88–89).

When we think of Jesus' words in relation to happiness, we miss the depth of what he's talking about because the blessing he promises, the joy he promises, is completely untouchable. It is totally unassailable by the world. In giving us the Beatitudes, Jesus is telling us that blessedness looks different from God's perspective. The world may tell us what it takes to bring happiness, but Jesus is telling us that the world's view may not be as accurate as we think. The joy God gives isn't tied to happenstance, chance, or change. It is deeper, more lasting, and may even have some surprising components.

God's joy and blessing are what God's kingdom is all about. Christ followers are Kingdom people. Christ followers are folks who are in relationship with God through Christ, who live in hope of eternal life and live out that hope in their daily lives, thus experiencing God's blessing and joy. The Beatitudes tell us what it means to be Kingdom people, to live in God's kingdom. They are concrete expressions of the nature of Kingdom life.

The Latin American Jesuit theologian Jon Sobrino described spirituality as a profound motivation; he said that it's about instincts, intuitions, longings and desires—both within nature and in our culture—that move us, inspire us and shape us, inform and fill our decisions and actions. That definition of *spirituality*—"profound motivation"—connects with Jesus' words to us to seek the kingdom of God first, and everything else will be added (see Matthew 6:33). Our spirituality is *whatever we desire most*. Whatever we strive for, whatever motivates us, drives us, moves us to select one thing over another; whatever primary shaping forces are in our life, that's our spirituality.

Following in the Jesus way is about recognizing that Jesus calls us to a particular type of spirituality, a way of life that's shaped by seeking and finding God's presence in our life, doing whatever is necessary to put God at the very center of our lives, to put ourselves at the very center of God's will. When we do that, we experience deep, abiding, life-changing, life-marking joy—not because we've earned it or achieved it, not because of chance or circumstance, but because it already exists. God's blessedness is already there, and we experience it when we seek God's kingdom. Jesus promised that when we seek the kingdom of God and God's righteousness first, everything else will be added. That adds up to a type of happiness the world can't give or take away.

My parents have a friend, Tammy, who graduated from Asbury Seminary. Converted to Christianity during her college years at the University of Georgia, she attended Asbury on faith, never knowing completely how she would pay for her education but trusting that God would provide, which God somehow always did. After participating in a short-term mission trip to South Asia, she returned there after she graduated in the late 1990s to establish Grace House, a home for children who are on the street. Her approach to Grace House is the same as was her approach to seminary—she depends totally on God; she never asks anyone for money, but God always seems to provide what her children need. By 2000, there were forty children in her care in two locations. Tammy understands what it means to follow in the Jesus way, putting herself at the center of God's will. She has sought God's kingdom first, and the happiness she has experienced can never be taken from her. In an e-mail to my father, she encouraged others to discover for themselves what she has found:

I encourage you to let God take you deeper in prayer and intimacy. I know these are the "Christian catch phrases" these days. But . . . well . . . it's the truth. I guess my prayer for you is that you would go deeper with Jesus, that you would let Him wash through you like a rushing river, cleansing, soothing, filling you in every good way. Intimacy . . . Just more of Jesus. That place where you utter a prayer and in an instant, you know it has been answered. That place where you are convicted of your self and sin and in the same moment, encouraged and refreshed. That place in your heart where man's words cannot reach, but one word from God, and you melt. (*The Workbook on Lessons from the Saints*, by Maxie D. Dunnam; Upper Room Books, 2002; page 160)

The biggest challenge for Christ followers who seek to follow Jesus side by side rather than at a distance is the implicit question of the Beatitudes: Will we yield ourselves totally to Jesus? Will we allow him to shape our lives and give us happiness, joy, and blessedness, or will we continue to seek happiness by following the direction of the world? When we yield ourselves to Jesus, following in the Jesus way—up close, in the thick of things, not at a distance and in the shadows—we experience the deep joy, fulfillment, and satisfaction that Tammy has experienced in her work in South Asia. We become Kingdom people.

But what do Kingdom people look like? Kingdom people look like Tammy. Yet, they also look like the man we discussed in chapter 3— the man Jesus healed and then sent back to his own town to tell of the great things God had done for him (Luke 8:26-39). Kingdom people come in different shapes and sizes, have different gifts and passions; they follow by leaving home and by staying put.

But Kingdom people have several important things in common, and the Beatitudes offer several aspects of Kingdom people that are worth noting. Kingdom people seek to live their lives in sync with God and thus receive God's blessing. They are poor in spirit, recognizing their intense need for God, understanding that they are not self-sufficient and therefore putting their whole trust in God. Kingdom people experience mourning, yet they are also blessed with Christ's healing comfort and peace. They understand that the deeper the love, the deeper the loss—and in that same moment they recognize that it was with the deepest love of all that Jesus offered himself up for them. Kingdom people hunger and thirst for righteousness, working for the full realization of God's kingdom in the world. They are merciful, extending forgiveness to others because they know forgiveness is crucial to God's justice, and because they're always aware of how much they've been forgiven. Kingdom people know that true children of God are peacemakers. They act as radical agents of love, which requires courage in a world whose foundation is force. When they are persecuted, Kingdom people continue to have hope, receiving God's blessing, which provides them comfort in the midst of suffering. They understand that their lives are lived in God's hand. They understand that God ultimately has won the victory, and they will share in God's reward. Not all Kingdom people experience persecution, but they all align themselves with those who do, with those who suffer, and they work to alleviate that suffering and end that persecution.

Kingdom people are humble; they are meek and lowly and gentle. That's a particularly difficult and challenging aspect of following in the Jesus way, and it is particularly significant in these times in which we find ourselves. The world doesn't reward meekness; that isn't an attribute that usually gets us to the top—and American society is all about getting to the top. Actually, American society is all about consuming—getting—but the reality is that people on the top get more. The more successful one is, the more one gets, the more one is able to consume, the better one can experience "the American dream."

Being gentle and lowly doesn't usually get a person very much. Jesus knew this when he talked about a particular experience he had at a dinner at which he was a guest. When Jesus arrived, he noticed that everyone was trying to get the best seat in the house. Everyone was intent on getting as close to the head of the table as possible. This observation prompted him to explain that we look at life backwards. We calculate that getting a better seat will aid us in advancing up the ladder of success—it will add to our honor. When *we* do the math, getting a better seat adds up to receiving greater honor.

Have you ever heard of "fuzzy math"? That's a question we used to open a worship experience a while back. I asked the congregation to participate in a simple math quiz: "What's $1 + 1$?" When they—especially the children—shouted, "Two," I informed them they were wrong, that $1 + 1 = 3$. When they told me that $2 + 4 = 6$, I said, "Wrong again! It's nine." Obviously I had a confused congregation on my hands, but they began to get the message about fuzzy math, the kind of math where the numbers don't quite add up right. Our call to worship continued: "Jesus practiced fuzzy math. In calculating how to get status in the kingdom, he advised that the best plan of action was one of humility, equality and inclusion: 'For all who exalt themselves will be humbled, and those who humble themselves will be exalted.' Let's learn together how to practice Kingdom math" (*Fuzzy Math*, 2001; Lumicon Digital Productions, Dallas, TX: mPower Pack worship experience).

Jesus' math is always fuzzy. He turns our assumptions around because he wants us to think as Kingdom people. He wants us to look at life from the perspective of the future of God's kingdom back into the present. In talking about his dinner experience, he says, "If you are invited to a wedding feast, don't always head for the best seat. . . . Do this instead—sit at the foot of the table. Then when your host sees you, he will come and say, 'Friend, we have a better place than this for you!' Then you will be honored in front of all the other guests. For the proud will be humbled, but the humble will be honored" (Luke 14:8, 10-11, NLT).

Jesus wants us to think about our place at the table in light of God's will and purpose. If we are Kingdom people, if we are following in the Jesus way, then we will think about what the Kingdom is going to be like—a place where those who have humbled themselves will be honored and those who have honored themselves in the kingdom of this world will be humbled. The idea of humbling ourselves now is a challenging notion, because we are often confused by our concept of self-esteem. We confuse humility, being humble or gentle or lowly, with low self-esteem. That's a sadly mistaken perception. Humility is not about low self-esteem. It is about accurate esteem, it is about Kingdom esteem. Humility involves understanding that our worth is not estimated by the world's calculations—that is, where we sit at the table. God's math is much fuzzier—our worth is calculated not from our place at the table but from our place in God's heart.

We are God's beloved creatures. We are made in God's image, paid for with the very life of God. We are creatures of unimaginable value, not because of our own merits—where we sit at the table, what we've accomplished, or how successful we are—but because we belong to God. God loves us unconditionally and without end, understanding that fact is what God-esteem—Kingdom-esteem—is all about. Kingdom-esteem leads to humility, because it involves recognizing that it's not about us, it's about what God has done for us.

But Jesus doesn't stop there when talking about humility. Humility doesn't simply involve what we think of ourselves. It is intimately connected to what we think about others, how we esteem them and relate to them, and how we show them hospitality. Hospitality in the Jesus way entails showing love to those who can't give us anything in return. Jesus said the crucial issue is not that we open our hearts and lives to folks who can repay us (see Luke 14:12); anybody can do that (Luke 6:33). The crucial issue is how we behave toward those who can do nothing for us (Luke 6:35; 14:13). Kingdom people, those who are following in the Jesus way, don't just open their hearts to those who can later provide them with some sort of benefit. They do not focus only on those who can show hospitality in return. Kingdom people show hospitality to everyone, particularly those who can do nothing in return. If we are following Jesus side by side, we'll be practicing fuzzy math rather than calculating things from the world's perspective. Kindness, love, hospitality toward those who can do something in return will certainly reap rewards right now. That kind of behavior will more than likely add up to our increased success. But love, concern, support, solidarity with those who can do nothing for us will reap even greater rewards for eternity.

In the fall of 2002, the nineteen-year-old son of a woman in my church participated in a violent crime in which he and another young man broke into a woman's home in search of drugs and money. They found the woman asleep on the couch, but she roused at their noise; and while my friend's son searched the kitchen, the other man bludgeoned the woman to death. Like so many events in our society, this one was a complex mix of tragedy on all sides. There was the obvious tragedy of violent death and its ensuing pain, suffering, anger, grief, and loss, mixed with the heartbreak of a life gone disastrously off course—mental illness, drug abuse, homelessness.

My friend's son asked to see me a few days after he was arrested, and thus began over a year of regular visits to our county jail, which continue at this writing. Ultimately he was sentenced to eighty-five years in prison. I spoke at his sentencing hearing about the depth of his remorse, about the hard spiritual work he had been doing and continues to do in order to accept responsibility for his actions and get his soul right with God. While I thoroughly believe that this young man has genuinely accepted responsibility for his part in this horrific event and is deeply remorseful, and while I am confident that God has worked in his life during his incarceration, truly making him a new and different person, speaking at the hearing was not an easy thing for me to do. My heart went out to the victim's daughter. My pastoral spirit desired to comfort her as well as my own friend and her son. It felt as if the eyes of all the court personnel—the victim's advocate, the prosecutor, the security officers—were all trained on me as if to say, "You're on the wrong side." The victim's family as well verbally expressed surprise that a pastor would stand on behalf of anyone involved in such a crime. Clearly, offering care and support to the victim's family would have resulted in a greater benefit for me, particularly from the perspective of newspaper reporting and public opinion. But my commitment to Christ is for eternity, and that is where my eyes were focused as I visited the jail and spoke in the courtroom.

Following in the Jesus way involves humility—an accurate sense of our Kingdom-esteem. As I sought to follow Jesus, Jesus put me right in the thick of things, so close to the fire that I felt the intensity of the heat in the eyes of everyone in the courtroom and at the jail. But Jesus became real to me, spoke to me in a little Pentecost moment, and enabled me to remember that he came not just to offer salvation to victims but—and especially—to perpetrators when they are truly repentant. I could follow then with an inner joy that had no connection to the tragic circumstances of which I was a part, knowing that my worth was secure, knowing that God's blessing was available, knowing that I was indeed a part of the Kingdom.

That's what following in the Jesus way is all about—experiencing joy, happiness, meaning, and strength, not just sporadically depending on what's going on in our lives but consistently and lastingly. It's about living as Kingdom people, recognizing that God's blessing exists right now, that joy can be ours—even when we suffer; especially when we struggle for justice; particularly when we are merciful, gentle, lowly, and humble. Joy can be ours when we place Christ at the center of our hearts and live as Kingdom people, following Jesus side by side, reversing the world's take on happiness and experiencing the deep and everlasting blessing that the world can never give nor take away.

Study / Discussion Questions

1. How might you be living out of the world's understanding of blessedness, rather than Jesus' understanding of blessedness?

2. Reflect on Jon Sobrino's description of spirituality as profound motivation, that our spirituality is "whatever we desire most." How does that description fit your life? What have you ordered your life around thus far—what do you desire most?

3. What might have to change in your life if you were to begin doing whatever is necessary to put God at the very center of your life, to put yourself at the very center of God's will? Make a brief list of some checkpoints.

4. How have you experienced the concepts of humility and accurate self-esteem in your life? What new insights have you gained during this time of reading and reflection?

5. How has your understanding of humility had an impact upon your behavior toward others? How might your behavior change as a result of this time of reading and reflection? Make note of some of those changes.

Focus for the Coming Week

Enter into a time of prayer, committing or recommitting yourself to living as a Kingdom person, with a renewed sense of God's blessing. Determine to implement at least one of the changes you listed above.

Prayer

Lord, please forgive me when my profound motivation is not you. Empower me to go deeper with you, live my life in sync with you. Open me to the reality of your blessing that I might yield myself completely to you, following you even when the fire becomes intense and the rewards seem far away. Amen.

Faith vs. Fear

Ahab reported to Jezebel everything that Elijah had done,
including the massacre of the prophets.
Jezebel immediately sent a messenger to Elijah
with her threat: "The gods will get you for this
and I'll get even with you! By this time tomorrow
you'll be as dead as any one of those prophets."
When Elijah saw how things were, he ran for dear life
to Beersheba, far in the south of Judah. He left his young
servant there and then went on into the desert another
day's journey. He came to a lone broom bush
and collapsed in its shade, wanting in the worst way
to be done with it all—to just die.
1 Kings 19:1-4 (THE MESSAGE)

Following Jesus is not an easy task. You probably knew that before you ever began this study, and I have emphasized that reality time and again. It is simply much easier to follow at a distance. There are many reasons for this, several of which we have already discussed. However, there is one distinct block that is particularly important to explore, especially as our time together begins to draw to a close.

If you recall Peter's experience in the courtyard, you'll remember that it was a very frightening time. Peter had experienced not a few dramatic events, all crammed into a short period of time. The Gospels record that Jesus had turned the Passover supper on its head with a foot-washing and predictions of betrayal and death. Judas had walked out on the entire project. Peter and the rest of the disciples had fallen asleep in the garden while Jesus was praying, which had led to yet another rebuke. Then Judas led a band of soldiers into the garden, confronting Jesus. Peter attacked the high priest's servant with his sword, cutting off the man's ear and prompting Jesus to heal one last time before they led him away. Finally Peter found himself standing in the courtyard, most likely scared to death. It is no wonder that he lurked in the shadows, away from the fire; fear is an incredible obstacle to faith. (See Matthew 26; Mark 14; Luke 22; John 13–18.)

Fear undermines. It blocks faith and achievement. It disrupts our life direction, hinders us from seeing God's picture of our lives and discovering our life mission. Peter was sidetracked by fear that night in the courtyard. So was Elijah when he fled the wrath of Jezebel.

Elijah was one of God's mighty prophets in the days of the Old Testament. In a time when the people of God were following at a comfortable distance, Elijah was following up close and in the thick of things. He stood with integrity and spoke with courage and boldness.

Elijah knew how to depend on God. God led him into hiding in the wilderness for his safety, fed him for an entire year with food carried by ravens, and then showed him the way to a widow who was able to provide him shelter from his enemies.

Elijah understood that God was in control. He had experienced the power of God working through him to resurrect a widow's son and bring fire to the altar when the priests of Baal were unable. Elijah was faithful, focused, and obedient, standing so close to the fire that he was in danger of being burned. And that is where fear enters the picture. (See 1 Kings 16:29—18:45.)

When we follow in the Jesus way, we will always encounter resistance. The fire can get very hot, and there will always be disruptive events that challenge our commitment to follow. That is what happened to Elijah. He had experienced great prophetic success; but even as he sought to be faithful to God, forces of resistance challenged him, bringing him to the end of his rope. Queen Jezebel had been systematically murdering the spiritual leaders of Israel, and now she set her sights directly on Elijah. He was terrified and ran for his life. (See 1 Kings 19:1-3.) His life direction was disrupted. He was sidetracked by fear.

I believe this is an experience common to all of us. We undergo spiritual growth and gain maturity in our devotion and success in our faith. We believe we are living out of our God picture, our life mission. But then the world throws resistance or disruption at us, or we experience a spiritual plateau, and suddenly we're paralyzed. The forward movement of our spiritual journey is halted.

I have a friend who is a wellspring of faith and encouragement. She attends our contemporary worship service and has been a significant source of spiritual mentoring for many people. One day, however, she stopped coming. I e-mailed her, wondering what was wrong. She would e-mail back occasionally, but she did not return to church. Over the course of several months, I lost contact with her altogether.

Finally, she contacted me, wanting to talk. We met; and as her story unfolded, it was clear to me that she was experiencing, among other things, an overarching spiritual paralysis. Despite the depth of her faith and the significance of her ministry in our church and our community, she doubted her place in the Kingdom. Her faith had been disrupted, and now she feared she wasn't "spiritual enough." Living in spiritual fear, she retreated from the community of faith— the very people who could support her and carry her through. The further she retreated, the greater the paralysis became.

My friend experienced spiritual fear and paralysis and dealt with it by retreating from the community of faith; Elijah experienced fear and paralysis and dealt with it by running away to a broom bush, and then to the dark depths of a cave on Mount Sinai (1 Kings 19:4-9a).

Humans have developed many tools to deal with fear. One of the first tools we make use of is control. When something bad happens to us, we exercise our feeling of control and do everything in our power to keep this bad thing from happening again. My friend exercised her feeling of control by retreating. Elijah exercised his feeling of control by running away. It's a basic human instinct. In the wonderful animated movie *Finding Nemo,* a clownfish, Marlin, experiences the tragic loss of his entire family in a barracuda attack. Only one tiny fish egg remains. As he holds the egg in his fins, Marlin says, "There, there, there, it's okay, Daddy's here; Daddy's got you. I promise I will never let anything happen to you . . . Nemo." Thus begins Marlin's quest to control every aspect of Nemo's life, to ensure his safety and "not let anything happen to him."

Control is a figment of our imaginations, a fact that Marlin quickly learns when Nemo is unexpectedly taken far from home. Even Dory, the forgetful regal-blue Tang fish who joins Marlin in his search for Nemo, recognizes how illusory our control truly is. When she and

Marlin are inside a whale and Marlin is ready to give up the search, he tells her of his promise never to let anything happen to Nemo. Dory's response is simply, "Huh, that's a funny thing to promise." Dory recognizes that there is no way to control life. Life unfolds regardless of our attempts to rein it in.

That is exactly what Elijah discovers. He had experienced great victories in his life, but now he finds himself in a state of fear and paralysis; he can't control the events unfolding around him. He's under the broom bush; he can't eat; he can't sleep; he is so fearful that he even asks God to end his life. When you get to this point, it's hard to hear God anymore. This was the case with my friend. She couldn't discern God's direction. She was filled with isolation and doubt.

Committing ourselves to the Jesus way does not mean that we will be spared moments of crisis like these—moments when we are filled with fear and paralysis. However, if we are to continue to follow side by side, rather than at a distance, we must be prepared and make use of the spiritual resources that God has provided. Elijah's experience helps us understand those resources.

Elijah has traveled from the broom bush to the depths of a cave on Mount Sinai. God finds him there and asks a very important question: "What are you doing here, Elijah?" (1 Kings 19:9b, NLT). It is as though God is asking, "Why would you come to this place after all I've done? Don't you remember my power? Don't you remember my love and care? What are you doing here so full of fear and doubt?"

God asks, but then God directs; and these directions provide us with insight. God offers Elijah, and us, three specific spiritual resources: *visioning, speaking,* and *acting.* As with our life picture, God desires us to have a faith picture. God wants us to have a vision of faith always before us. God tells Elijah, "Go out and stand before me on the mountain" (1 Kings 19:11, NLT). When we talk about life-changing experiences, moments that have such a great impact on us that we can never forget them, we often describe them as "mountaintop experiences." This is because mountains are places of vision. Our sightlines are expanded when we stand on a mountain. Our perspective changes when we view our surroundings from a mountaintop. When Elijah stood on the mountain, the Lord passed by; and Elijah was given a renewed vision of faith.

Just as recognizing God's picture for our lives can be difficult because we focus on our limitations, envisioning faith is difficult because we limit ourselves to what is visible at any given time. But that is not what faith is all about. Hebrews 11:1 tells us that "faith is being sure of what we hope for and certain of what we do not see" (NIV). "It is the confident assurance that what we hope for is going to happen. It is the evidence of things we cannot yet see" (NLT).

Faith isn't about the reality we perceive around us. It's about the reality of the unseen presence and promise of God. When we reach points of difficulty and resistance on our faith journey, when we become fearful and paralyzed, our inclination is to focus on the visible. Elijah was focusing on the circumstances that surrounded him. Jezebel had threatened him, and she had the resources to carry out that threat as was evidenced by the visible bodies of those she had ordered killed. In *Finding Nemo*, Marlin was focused on the visible circumstances of loss—the loss of his wife and their future children, the loss of Nemo, and then on the visible circumstances of being seemingly trapped inside a whale. Our inclination is to focus on the visible, and in doing so, we remove ourselves and begin following at a distance. But following in the Jesus way is not about the visible. It's about the invisible promise of God. It's about realizing that nothing has changed, even though our circumstances might lead us to believe it has. God's promise continues to be valid; God is still present with us. Everything that God has envisioned for our lives remains intact.

When God made the covenant with the Israelites, gave them the law, and was preparing them to enter the Promised Land, God spoke these words through Moses: "Watch out! Be very careful never to forget what you have seen the LORD do for you. Do not let these things escape from your mind as long as you live! And be sure to pass them on to your children and grandchildren" (Deuteronomy 4:9, NLT). God's message is that it is the Israelites' faith picture that will sustain them in their new land. It is their commitment to keeping that vision of faith ever before them that will make or break their experience as God's people. The biblical witness shows how important this spiritual resource is. When difficulties arose for the Israelites, the strength of their faith picture was always a crucial ingredient to the outcome. More often than not, when they lost their vision of faith, when they forgot what the Lord had done for them, their difficulties increased and calamity followed.

Keeping a vision of faith before us is critical if we are to follow in the Jesus way. As I talked to my friend, I had to remind her of her faith picture. I had to evoke her vision of faith: *Remember what God has done for you. God is still here. Your community of faith is still here. Nothing has changed. God hasn't revoked God's promise. God still loves you and has plans and life pictures for you.* Keeping our vision of faith in the forefront is crucial. We have to continually shape it and form it and articulate it in order to push through the times of resistance and disruption. God's words to the Israelites are also for us:

> You must commit yourselves wholeheartedly to these commands I am giving you today. Repeat them again and again to your children. Talk about them when you are at home and when you are away on a journey, when you are lying down and when you are getting up again. Tie them to your hands as a reminder, and wear them on your forehead. Write them on the doorposts of your house and on your gates.
> (Deuteronomy 6:6-9, NLT)

As we rehearse our vision of faith over and over, keeping it ever before us, it strengthens and sustains us, remaining intact as a source of strength during times of crisis and resistance.

Let's return to Elijah. He obeyed God's command and stood on Mount Sinai; and as he stood in that place of vision, he encountered God. It was an intense experience. There was a mighty windstorm; the wind was so strong that it broke rocks from the mountain. There was an earthquake. There was a fire. Then there was a whisper (1 Kings 19:11-13). Envisioning faith, keeping that picture in front of us, requires attending to aspects of life that aren't readily apparent. God wasn't in the wind, wasn't in the earthquake, and wasn't in the fire. God was found in that "still small voice" (1 Kings 19:12, RSV).

The voice of God is not always readily noticeable. It is not something we always have an ear for. Yet following in the Jesus way involves attending to things that aren't readily apparent. It involves listening for the voice of God and placing ourselves in a position to hear it regularly and often. My Belgian friend Mieke has lived in the United States for many years. She recently participated in a program that required her to ride along with a local police officer during an eight-hour shift. During her ride along, she encountered a police dog and heard the officer giving the dog commands—in Dutch! As she relayed the story, she exclaimed, "It was a Belgian dog!" I laughed because the thought occurred to me that here was a *dog* that could comprehend a language that I am completely unable to understand. A similar thought occurs to me every time I visit Mieke's family and hear them conversing happily in Flemish—especially the children. Here I am, an educated adult, and I can't understand a word they are saying; yet there they are—four-year-olds!—and they have no problem understanding whatsoever.

I understand that I speak English because I grew up in an English-speaking home. Mieke speaks Flemish because she grew up in Belgium, in a Flemish-speaking home. The police dog understood Dutch because its handlers, those who trained it from its earliest memory, spoke Dutch. We recognize the voices, the language, of those with whom we surround ourselves. We speak whatever language we hear regularly and often. If we are to hear the voice of God, and thus have an understanding of what it means to follow Jesus in real time, we must surround ourselves with the language and voice of God. We must hang out in places where God's voice can be heard regularly and often.

My sister and mother are artists; I am not, but I do enjoy creating jewelry. A strange thing happens when I am around my mother and sister. I begin to feel more creative. I become excited about creating something beautiful with my pliers and silver and beads; and I'll often return from a visit and produce five or six pieces in a flurry of activity. But as time passes, my creative energy often wanes; and I will go for weeks without creating anything.

If we desire to be creative, to nurture that part of ourselves consistently rather than sporadically, it helps to hang out with creative people—to see people who are further along on their artistic journey. If we desire to attend to the things that aren't readily apparent, to hear the voice of God that molds and shapes our vision of faith, we must hang out in places where God's voice can be heard, where we can consistently see people who are further along on their journey of faith and can energize us to push through in times of disruption and paralysis.

God offers Elijah the spiritual resource of faith visioning in order to help him push through his state of paralysis and follow more closely: "Stand before me on the mountain." Then God offers another directive: "Speak." God tells Elijah to find Hazael, Jehu, and Elisha and tell them about what he has experienced, anointing Hazael and Jehu as kings and Elisha as the next prophet. God's directive to speak is a significant directive if we are going to push through our difficulties in order to follow in the Jesus way.

In the movie *The Italian Job,* a group of sophisticated thieves coordinate their talents to steal millions of dollars worth of gold bars. Each has a particular skill that he or she brings to the group, along with a creative nickname. One thief, Lyle, is a computer genius who wants the others to call him "The Napster," insisting that he invented the downloading software that revolutionized the Internet and changed the face of the music industry. He maintains that his college roommate stole the idea from him, claimed it as his own, and went on to make millions. His colleagues in crime scoff at his assertion, pointing to the reality that someone else was ultimately responsible for Napster; of course, when Lyle proves himself to be a computer genius, contributing mightily to the success of their heist, they put their skepticism aside and readily oblige his nickname request.

This is a silly example of an important truth: If we hold an idea or belief within ourselves, it will always remain an idea; it can never become a reality. Only by speaking our idea or belief aloud, by sharing it with others, is it empowered to become a reality. In speaking, we give life to our ideas and beliefs; they begin to exist outside ourselves, becoming infectious and dynamic. That is why the apostle Paul included both speaking and believing in his instructions to the Romans: "For if you confess with your mouth that Jesus is Lord and believe in your heart that God raised him from the dead, you will be saved. For it is by believing in your heart that you are made right with God, and it is by confessing with your mouth that you are saved" (Romans 10:9-10, NLT).

Like the experience of many of us, my adolescence was rocky and difficult. My classmates spoke resistance and disruption: "Nerd," "Brain," "Loser"; but my mother always spoke faith: "Your day will come, you will shine, you will blossom, you will flourish." She was like Moses in the wilderness. There was adversity all around, worries about water, about food. But Moses never spoke about adversity; he spoke about the land that God had promised, a land flowing with milk and honey.

Speaking faith *grows* faith. It creates and solidifies our faith visions and those of others around us. It enables Jesus to work through us to work miracles in the lives of those around us. It moves us forward through adversity, fear, paralysis, and resistance to keep us following

Jesus side by side rather than dropping back to a distance. When we speak, we make ourselves accountable. We expand our sense of following from a solely internal project to an external one. As we speak faith, the vision we place beyond ourselves takes on a life of its own; it becomes infectious and dynamic.

Many of us decide to give up something during the Lenten season, a sacrifice we choose to make as we enter this significant time of reflection and following Jesus on his journey to the cross. I usually choose to give up my favorite soft drink, which is Diet Coke. I have learned over the years that if I keep this commitment to myself, telling no one, it becomes very easy to fall short, because if I slip up no one knows. That's why I tell my family and close friends about my Lenten sacrifice—not to boast about my self-denial but to hold myself accountable. My idea to give up this thing I enjoy becomes a reality when I speak about it with others. They now latch on to the idea and hold me accountable to my commitment. I don't dare slip up! The idea to undertake an element of self-denial takes on a life of its own when I speak it aloud. It becomes infectious and dynamic, even influencing my youngest daughter to make it part of her Lenten experience as well.

Becoming a Christ follower isn't just about attending church, showing up once a week to sit and listen. Coming to sit and listen may enable you to attend to part of Paul's instruction—believing in your heart. But it will not satisfy all of his instruction—confessing with your mouth. That's why we include a public declaration when we receive new members into the community of faith. When we stand up and proclaim our faith, it becomes dynamic. Speaking our faith brings life to the idea of our belief, moving it outside our selves. It requires that we move beyond the privacy of our internal spirituality, where no one knows about our commitment and no one can hold us accountable to it. Speaking faith keeps us close to the fire, enabling us to follow Jesus side by side even through periods of paralysis and fear.

Elijah received three spiritual resources to aid him in pressing on despite his fear and spiritual paralysis. God asks him, Why are you here? And then instructs Elijah to stand before God on the mountain—to *envision* his faith. God also instructs Elijah to tell three others about his experience with God—to *speak* his faith. God asks Elijah a second time, "What are you doing here?" (1 Kings 19:13, NLT). I believe that

58

is a question for all of us. The fact that you are participating in this study indicates a partial answer to that question. You desire to follow Jesus more intimately; you are seeking a closer connection to God. God's third instruction to Elijah is significant for us: *Act* on faith. God tells Elijah to go back the way he came (1 Kings 19:15).

We cannot follow in the Jesus way until we act. Returning to Peter, he was transformed each time he acted on what he knew in that moment. Bit by bit, Peter's actions of faith shaped and molded him into the true person God intended him to be—when he stepped out of the boat at the call of Jesus during a storm (Matthew 14:22-33; when he declared Jesus to be the Christ, the Son of the living God, at Caesarea-Philippi (Matthew 16:13-19); and when he began to preach to the crowds of Jerusalem (Acts 2:14-42). Holy-Spirit power flowed though Peter when he acted on what he knew—offering the love of the resurrected Christ to all those who had rejected the earthly Jesus. Peter did not need to know it all, but he did need to act on whatever he knew at the time; and when he did so, his life was transformed.

Following Jesus up close, rather than at a distance, involves basing our lives on the reality of faith rather than the reality of fear. We serve an awesome God, a God whose promises are steadfast and whose presence, while unseen, is everlasting. When we keep that vision of faith before us, when we declare our faith aloud giving it a life of its own, when we act on whatever faith God has provided us in the moment, we move to Jesus' side; and we are able to walk with him in intimacy and power.

Study / Discussion Questions

1. What disruptions have you experienced in your faith walk where your forward motion of faith was stalled? Describe them briefly.

2. How have you attempted to exercise control in your life?

3. Reflect on your faith picture, on those who have provided it for you, and the ways in which you keep it before you. Have you experienced the block of focusing only on the visible? If so, how has that experience played out in your life? What has been helpful in enabling you to continually rehearse your vision of faith?

4. Think about your ability to attend to things of God that aren't readily apparent. Have you made use of this spiritual resource to help you keep your faith picture alive and vibrant? Why or why not?

5. Are you regularly placing yourself in environments that are conducive to hearing God's voice? Are you surrounding yourself with others who are further along on their journey in order to be energized and encouraged in times of disruption and paralysis? Why or why not?

6. How might *speaking* faith make you more accountable in your spiritual walk? Make some notes about your thoughts.

Focus for the Coming Week

This week, focus on ways in which you might act on what you know at this moment in your faith journey. Remember that you do not have to know it all; there are courses of action perfectly fit for your current faith location. Resolve to incorporate *visioning* faith, *speaking* faith, and *acting* faith as you follow Jesus.

Prayer

Forgive me, Lord, for focusing on the visible rather than on your invisible but everlasting presence in my life. Empower me to keep my faith ever before me, to speak it continuously and to act on it as I seek to follow you with intimacy. Guard me from the paralysis of fear, and loose its bonds on me that I might be free to continue my journey with you. Amen.

Singleness of Heart

*"God blesses those whose hearts are pure,
for they will see God."*
Matthew 5:8 (NLT)

*If you do away with the yoke of oppression, / with the
pointing finger and malicious talk, / and if you spend
yourselves in behalf of the hungry / and satisfy the needs
of the oppressed, / then your light will rise in the darkness, /
and your night will become like the noonday.*
Isaiah 58:9-10 (NIV)

As we come nearer to the end of our time together, we return to a Beatitude that is particularly significant as we seek to follow Jesus in a more intimate way: "God blesses those whose hearts are pure, / for they will see God" (Matthew 5:8, NLT). The importance of our hearts cannot be overestimated. Life itself is a matter of the heart. Our entire life, from birth to death, is a journey of heart development. With each passing day our characters are molded and our souls enlarged until we come to stand before God. This journey is a matter of the heart because our heart is the very center of ourselves. It is our heart that shapes our character. The way we often describe others is an indicator of the importance of our hearts. Some of us have brave hearts, others have faint hearts; there are cheating hearts and generous hearts; we have all met folks who are hard-hearted and those with gentle, tender hearts as well. Our hearts are also integral to our emotions, rendering us warmhearted or cold. Our will is intimately connected to our hearts every time we steel our hearts for a particularly difficult event or decision.

Our moral integrity is thoroughly tied to our hearts because from our hearts flow the good, the bad, and everything in between.

As we seek to follow in the Jesus way, everything is a matter of the heart, which makes the condition of our heart absolutely crucial. What's more, our heart is the place in which Christ lives through the power of the Holy Spirit; thus our hearts guide us in following Jesus in real time. Because of this, God's Word from Proverbs is significant: "Above all else, guard your heart, / for it is the wellspring of life" (Proverbs 4:23, NIV).

The condition of our heart is critical to our ability to follow in the Jesus way; and it is clear that if we are to see God, if we are to experience the climax of our faith journey in full—standing face to face before this awesome God we follow, we must have pure hearts. Unfortunately, purity is a difficult concept to relate to in our day and age. One difficulty is that we associate it with cleanliness and perfection, with virtue and innocence—concepts that are overwhelming in their own right. The dictionary uses defining terms such as "unmixed," "homogeneous," "free of adulterants." Basically, *pure* means 100 percent of one thing. We may understand that idea, but another difficulty arises when we try to apply it or relate to it. The problem is that we have come to use the word *pure* very loosely. We are used to the fact that "pure" doesn't really mean *pure*. When we buy products that are labeled "pure" or "100 percent," we don't really believe that claim, because the fine print tells us otherwise. We know that 100 percent grape or orange juice is actually going to contain not just juice but a decent amount of water. Clearly, that's not 100 percent; it is not unmixed. In the reality of our world, *pure* no longer means "pure"; 100 percent is not really 100 percent.

While the word *pure* has come to have less and less meaning for the reality of our lives, it remains an important concept if we are going to follow in the Jesus way. We are made in the image of God. God created us to be whole, genuine (meaning "the real thing") persons. God desires that our hearts, the core of who we are, be pure. Remember the dictionary definition of *pure*—"having a homogeneous or uniform composition, not mixed" (*Webster's II New College Dictionary*, Houghton Mifflin Company, 2001). If we are to be genuine (the real thing) as we were created to be, our hearts must be undivided, undiluted, full-strength. That is the kind of heart needed if we are to follow Jesus side by side rather than at a distance.

Unfortunately, our hearts are anything but undivided. Thankfully we aren't alone in this difficulty. Peter and the rest of the disciples were challenged in this arena as well. They desired to follow Jesus, but their hearts were divided by their notion of what a Messiah was supposed to be and do. Their concept of Messiah as triumphant king hindered them from welcoming the leadership of a suffering servant with an undivided heart. They sought to follow Jesus, but their desire to sit in the favored spot in God's kingdom hindered them from taking up their own crosses with a singleness of heart.

We are not unlike the disciples. We struggle to follow Jesus with a singleness of heart, but our hearts are not undivided. Our hearts are actually a lot like icebergs. A small part is visible above the surface. That's our public heart, the heart we share with others, the heart we don't mind if people see and get to know. That is the part of us we are proud of; particularly in the context of faith, that is the part we willingly expose—our churchgoing, our Sunday-school participation, our piety. Then there is the part that is invisible, below the surface, our private heart—the part of our heart where we hide all the things we don't want anyone to see or know about, particularly God. If you've ever seen a picture of an iceberg, the submerged part is usually much bigger, wider, and deeper than the visible part. That was the hidden danger that caused the demise of the *Titanic*. The *Titanic*, the ship so many thought was unsinkable, narrowly missed an iceberg—or so everyone above deck thought—until they realized that the submerged part of the iceberg had ripped a fatal hole deep in the bowels of the ship.

Our hearts are much the same, and this can often produce similar results. There are things within our hearts that we submerge—all kinds of attitudes, passions, desires, behaviors—so that this unseen part grows and swells, getting wider and deeper, a menacing presence lurking below the surface. Then, when we encounter resistance in our faith walk or in our relationships, or when situations become "too close for comfort," we run the risk of all those things below the surface ripping us and others apart.

In chapter 4, I mentioned Jon Sobrino's concept of spirituality as profound motivation. Our spirituality is defined by whatever we desire most. If Sobrino is on target in his description of spirituality, it holds great significance for us as we seek to follow Jesus with an undivided heart. What is it that we desire most? Whatever it is, that becomes our spirituality. If it is not Christ, then we will be unable to follow with singleness of heart. Our spirituality will no longer be Christ-centered but centered on whatever it is that holds the attention of our hearts. When that occurs, we drop back to a distance, no longer following in the Jesus way with full strength and power.

In Isaiah 58, the prophet is attempting to get God's people to understand the truth to which Sobrino is pointing. The people believe that they are following in God's way. They seem to be seeking God out; and they claim to fast and humble themselves, eager for God to come near. Yet that is simply the visible part of the iceberg. Deep down their profound motivation is something other than being in relationship with God. They are living with divided hearts. On the surface they appear devout, yet they oppress their workers and ignore the needs of the hungry. Their fasting is not genuine, their humility not pure. Isaiah calls them to task:

Is not this the kind of fasting I have chosen:
to loose the chains of injustice
    and untie the cords of the yoke,
to set the oppressed free
    and break every yoke?
Is it not to share your food with the hungry
    and to provide the poor wanderer with shelter—
when you see the naked, to clothe him,
    and not to turn away from your own flesh and blood?
                                 (Isaiah 58:6-7, NIV)

The crux point of the chapter comes in verses 9-10, where Isaiah proclaims the power available when we follow God with a singleness of heart:

If you do away with the yoke of oppression,
    with the pointing finger and malicious talk,
and if you spend yourselves in behalf of the hungry
    and satisfy the needs of the oppressed,
then your light will rise in the darkness,
    and your night will become like the noonday. (NIV)

Isaiah's word for us is about the power we have when we follow in the Jesus way with an undivided heart, carrying out the ministry and mission of God in our world single-mindedly. We will be able to live in the light, righteousness will go before us, and God's glory will be our rear guard. God will be ever present to help us in our moments of need and struggle.

I believe the New International Version's choice of wording in verse 10 is significant. It says, "If you *spend* [italics added] your-selves. . . . " That's a telling word, particularly in relation to American culture. That's one thing Americans do very well—spend. We are a consumer culture. The question for us as we seek to follow Jesus side by side is, What are we spending ourselves on? How you answer that question is a major indicator of whether you are following Jesus with an undivided heart.

Paul described Christ followers as having the mind of Christ. Following in the Jesus way with singleness of heart is about aligning our thinking with God's thinking, our heart with God's heart. That is difficult, because we don't often think the same way God does. We seldom have an undivided heart, because our profound motivation is often not Christ; our thinking is not in sync with God's thinking. We may create the illusion that it is, we may decorate the visible part of the iceberg with the trappings of religious behavior, but the sub-merged portion reflects what we are truly spending ourselves on—not in following in the Jesus way but in the service of all sorts of other gods.

Every culture creates gods in order to justify its way of thinking and make people feel more comfortable about its lifestyle. Some preachers call them "feel-good gods." These feel-good gods divide our hearts and dilute our loyalty to living in the Jesus way. In the latter part of my grandparents' lives, they couldn't get out to church very often, so they'd watch television preachers. Television preachers are every-where. Many of them are wonderful, but many of them are not. Some of those with less integrity preach loyalty to feel-good gods, gods who after receiving a special monetary offering will bless you or heal you or make you rich. There are two misunderstood ideas that work to divide our hearts, to keep us from taking up our cross and following Jesus side by side. The first is personal peace. We believe that if we accept Jesus, we will find personal peace. Our profound motivation is not to follow Jesus into the thick of things but to experience per-sonal peace. The second misunderstood idea relates to affluence. We connect God's blessings to success and affluence, and our profound motivation ceases to be denying ourselves, taking up our cross, and following Jesus. Instead, it becomes experiencing success and affluence. We spend ourselves on the things that will contribute to our success and affluence.

God is sending us a wake-up call in Isaiah 58. We don't truly understand why God might be displeased. We feel as though we are following with singleness of heart: We go to church, we read the Bible. But when we leave the sanctuary, a different side emerges. It's that iceberg thing—all those things we don't want others to see. Isaiah names a few of them—oppression, indifference to the hungry, gossip, self-righteous judgment. Our hearts are divided because we are looking for a god who can give us personal peace and affluence, a god who can make us look good and feel good—even if it's at the expense of someone else.

The truth that is difficult and sometimes painful to accept is that following in the Jesus way is often not at all about personal peace. Matthew even says that Jesus didn't come to bring peace; he came to bring a sword (Matthew 10:34). In other words, if you are following in the Jesus way with singleness of heart, you are not likely to experience peace. You're more likely to experience tension—tension between the world's way and the Jesus way, the way the world encourages you to spend yourself and the way Jesus calls you to spend yourself. Certainly Jesus provides us with comfort and peace when we are in need; but the key is that we are in need—we are afflicted. As the cliché goes, Jesus comforts the afflicted and afflicts the comfortable. When I began exploring my faith in a deliberate way, I liked my world, I was content; but the more serious I got about following Jesus, the more displeasure I experienced. I was no longer content with the way things were in the world. I knew that God had a different dream, and I wanted to become engaged in making God's dream a reality.

A problem that divides our hearts is our confusion over commitment. We condense it to surface activity. Isaiah highlights this when he talks about fasting: "You humble yourselves by going through the motions of penance, bowing your heads like a blade of grass in the wind. You dress in sackcloth and cover yourselves with ashes. Is this what you call fasting? Do you really think this will please the LORD?" (Isaiah 58:5, NLT). Our worship can be the same way; we often have a completely different view of worship than the one Jesus held. For

Jesus, worship was sacrifice. Many of us participate in worship; we sing songs, recite liturgy. But where is the sacrifice? What is the cost of our words and our music? Paul asserted that "the kingdom of God is not just fancy talk; it is living by God's power" (1 Corinthians 4:20, NLT). It's not just a matter of coming to church once a week and reciting words and singing songs.

When we make a commitment to Jesus, we receive power. However, that power is not to be used to escape to our sanctuaries or worship spaces. It's not about a comfortable feeling of self-righteousness because others see us each week in church. It's not about maintaining the appearance of the top of our icebergs. Recall our discussion of Madonna's video for "Like a Prayer" from chapter 2. Jesus in real time breaks the chains of the past to go out into the world. Our relationship with Jesus, then, is not about escaping into comfort or personal peace; it's not about maintaining the image of our icebergs. It's about engagement. It's about going out into the world.

To follow in the Jesus way is to be sent out like the disciples in Luke 9. Jesus gave them power and authority to drive out all demons and heal all diseases. Then he sent them out with the understanding that they would take on the world—engage it and connect with it. He empowered them to confront the evil in the world, to be a source of healing in the lives of all they met. His instructions were specific. They weren't to take anything with them—no bag, no money, not even a walking stick. While we might prefer Samsonite, American Express, and a minivan with leather interior, that's not the Jesus way. Jesus wants us to travel light because it keeps our hearts undivided. Traveling light protects us against being weighed down by all our stuff; it's a way of guarding our hearts so that we won't become distracted, so that we'll be able to follow with a singleness of heart—keeping the main thing *the main thing*. Luke tells us that the disciples did as Jesus told them. They traveled light as they went from village to village, preaching the gospel and bringing healing to all they encountered.

Following in the Jesus way with an undivided heart is about engaging the needs of the world, not about surface activity. Jesus was not fond of "temple religion"—that self-righteous, counterfeit rehearsal of religious faith. In fact, Jesus was never a big hit in the Temple—that was where he seemed to get into the most trouble as he confronted the scribes and Pharisees who had sought to take the heart out of the law. For Jesus, what happened in the sanctuary, while important, wasn't nearly as significant as what happened in the street. Jesus broke the chains created by those who wished to keep God only in the sanctuary, and he embodied God's presence in the streets. He met folks where they were.

Our hearts become divided when we confuse "temple religion"—that surface-level practice of our faith—with our commitment to Christ, when we believe we are following through the flurry of our religious activity, when we believe we are following because the visible part of our iceberg *looks* like we're following. It's the activity that becomes our focus; it's the appearance. An undivided heart, however, recognizes that it's not about flurries of religious activity. It's about doing justice and giving mercy (Micah 6:8). Jesus promised that God blesses those with pure, undivided hearts, those whose profound motivation is following Christ. He promised that they will see God. He also described what those people look like. He said that those who follow with a singleness of heart are those who feed the hungry, give drink to the thirsty and clothes to the naked, visit the sick and imprisoned, and welcome the stranger. Following Jesus with an undivided heart means engaging the world on his behalf. It means getting in touch with the needs of the world—needs that can't always be placed in tidy categories, needs that sometimes require that we get dirty and even risk our reputations as "good church people."

As risky as all this sounds, the significant message that Isaiah provides us relates to cause and effect. Isaiah is saying, "God will give you power, not through your surface religious activities. Your power comes through your actions toward people." There is a distinct pattern of cause and effect in Isaiah's words; it's an "if-then" situation. "If you spend yourselves . . . then your light will rise." *If* you feed the hungry, work to free the oppressed, reach out to those in need; *if* you stop gossiping and put an end to self-righteousness, *then* your light will shine out from the darkness; *then* God will guide you and satisfy your needs and give you the power to flourish.

A few years ago, Isaiah's words hit home with me through an experience in my local church. A significant controversy arose over a particular woman's co-leadership of our annual vacation Bible school. This woman had been convicted of a crime and had served several years in a state prison. Having completed her sentence, she was released with no further legal requirements. While this was a difficult experience for her, her faith was solidified. She had joined our church some time after her release and was active in Bible study and other ministries. Her crime was unrelated to working with children, so the pastoral staff saw no danger in allowing her to volunteer for a co-coordinating position for our one-week VBS, a position in which she would be working in the company of others. While many people supported this woman in ministry, a small handful, including one person who was no longer a part of the congregation, did not. These individuals expressed concern, not necessarily for the VBS ministry but for the church's reputation; and they created quite an uproar. One, in particular, spoke to me directly, stating that it was okay if this woman worshiped with us. She could come to our picnics and participate in our Bible studies, but allowing her to lead was "dangerous for our reputation." Suddenly I understood the outrage God must have felt and expressed through Isaiah. My heart broke that those whom I was charged with guiding could be so unaware of the true nature of the gospel. I responded that the only reputation that matters for the people of God is our reputation for being a place of reconciliation, a place where people can come to receive a second chance, a place for forgiveness, acceptance, and love. The only reputation that matters for the people of God is the reputation we have for pouring ourselves out for others.

Some of us believe that we are being faithful to God simply because we come to church each week. We believe this shows that our hearts are undivided, that we are following in the Jesus way. I believe we are mistaken in that notion. It is through our actions with people that we receive our power. It is when we move out of our comfort zones, take risks, engage needs that we enter the realm of following in the Jesus way.

I have heard others use the metaphor of a squeezed-out grape to illustrate the sacrifice we celebrate in Communion. I believe that metaphor is appropriate here. Making our lives comfortable isn't God's top priority; neither is enhancing our reputations or helping us achieve success or affluence. God is about the business of squeezing us so that we can become drink—nourishment for the world. What I learned during my church's controversy is that too many of us are like marbles rather than grapes. If you try to squeeze a marble, more often than not it will slip out of your fingers, escape your grasp. We can be like marbles, trying to escape God's squeeze.

American culture is a climbing culture. We climb the ladder of success, and there is always something bigger to achieve, always more to get. Until the recent threat of lawsuits in the fast-food industry, the key word was *supersize*. We want to supersize it—move up to bigger cars, bigger houses. Peter succumbed to this temptation. When he climbed the mountain with Jesus, John, and James, he experienced the incredible presence of Moses and Elijah and heard God's voice pronouncing blessing on Jesus. His reaction was, "Let's build some shrines up here!" In other words, "Let's stay up here for a while and do something *big*!" But Jesus told him that they couldn't stay on the mountain. They had to go back down—down to the valley, where life happens.

Our world is focused on climbing, ascending mountains; but that's a sharp contrast to following in the Jesus way, which is about descending. When we follow Jesus with a singleness of heart, we are given the power to descend, down where the people are, down where it's dirty and messy. Following Jesus side by side requires that we leave our beautiful sanctuaries and worship spaces and begin spending ourselves on others—to feed the hungry, to help those in trouble, to engage, to risk our reputations, to reach out in forgiveness, to descend to the place where the people are.

When God calls, God's people are supposed to go. Those following at full strength, undiluted and undivided, aren't the ones who show up on Sunday and say "yes Lord" but then don't go. They are the ones who allow God to squeeze them like grapes, who allow themselves to stay in God's hands so they can be squeezed out as sustenance for the world. Those are the ones who will see God.

Study / Discussion Questions

1. How is your heart like an iceberg? What areas of your heart are visible above the surface? What do you keep hidden below? Make some notes to get a clear picture of the condition of your heart.

2. Make a list of the things you are "spending yourself" on. Be honest with yourself and with God.

3. Look at your list of the things you are spending yourself on. What does it say about your most profound motivation? What does it say about how well your thinking is aligned with God's thinking?

4. Reflect on the author's assertion that following in the Jesus way

is often not about personal peace. Specifically, focus on the statement, "If you are following in the Jesus way with singleness of heart, you are not likely to experience peace. You're more likely to experience tension—tension between the world's way and the Jesus way, the way the world encourages you to spend yourself and the way Jesus calls you to spend yourself." What insights into your own life has your reflection or discussion provided?

5. Reflect on your current commitment to Christ. Does it suggest surface activity or real engagement with the world, and how or why?

6. What would have to change in your life for you to become more like a squeezed-out grape, offering sustenance and nourishment to others? List those changes.

Focus for the Coming Week

This week, claim the power available through your actions toward people. Commit yourself to implementing one of the changes you have identified that you need to make in your life.

Prayer

Lord, create in me a clean heart, and guard me against internal division that would have me follow only on the surface. Please forgive me when I have confused the appearance of religious activity with deeper commitment, and empower me to spend myself on those things that are pleasing to you and that further your Kingdom. Amen.

Blood, Sweat, and Tears

He prayed more fervently, and he was in such agony
of spirit that his sweat fell to the ground
like great drops of blood.

Luke 22:44 (NLT)

We began our time together in the courtyard with Peter, the events of Jesus' passion unfolding at a terrifying rate around him. It's fitting that as we close our time together here in the Lenten season, we return to those events once more. As Jesus entered Jerusalem, surrounded by the smiles and cheers of folks waving palm branches and welcoming him warmly, it must have been easy for the disciples to think they had "arrived." This was it!

One of our dear friends is a former Big Ten Conference basketball coach. During his tenure, we had the pleasure of traveling with the team to various games and tournaments. On one occasion as we got off the bus, we were greeted by a throng of cheering fans. They were on both sides of the walkway into the building, smiling and cheering excitedly. As we all walked in together, I thought to myself, *Wow! I'm part of the group these folks are cheering for! This is it! This is really something!* It was an exhilarating experience. I imagine Peter must have felt something like that. *I'm part of the group these folks are cheering for! I'm with Jesus! In fact, I'm his right-hand man!*

The problem was that the trip wasn't really over. Peter *hadn't* arrived; he wasn't really there yet. The hard work was about to begin; the Passion was about to unfold, and Peter and the others were about to meet the real challenge.

As we follow Jesus, it's easy to get caught up in the excitement. We love the celebration. We love all the high moments, when everything fits together and seems right. You can see this in the way we mark the church calendar. Palm Sunday is the Sunday before Easter. It's also known as Passion Sunday, from the Latin word *passio,* which means "suffering," because it marks the beginning of Jesus' passion, the sufferings he experienced in Holy Week, his last week on earth. But few churches highlight Passion Sunday. Instead, they celebrate Palm Sunday. It's much more enjoyable to wave palms and sing hosannas than it is to take a good look at Jesus' suffering and death. It's as though we'd rather jump over Holy Week—Passion Week—and go straight from Palm Sunday to Easter without even blinking. Ironically, where we want to speed things up—get on with our Easter celebration—is right where the Gospels slow things down. In fact, almost half of the entire Gospel of John is devoted to the events of the last week of Jesus' life. Clearly, the Passion, Jesus' last week on earth, is something we need to attend to.

People tend to consider me a passionate person. Maybe that's why I love the word *passion.* In an English meaning of the word, *passion* means to be fully engaged. The thesaurus lists the opposites of *passion* as *indifference* or *casual interest.* That's because *passion* means to be committed with everything you've got. If you are passionate about something, *all* of you is wrapped up in it. We are inspired by passionate people. As we look at our lives, usually the people who have had the most profound impact on us were passionate people. It's passionate people who give the world symphonies and beautiful pieces of art. Our favorite books were written by passionate people. People of passion invent life-changing tools, discover life-enhancing medicines, and solve human problems. Passionate people aren't conformers. They aren't casually interested. They are completely immersed and give from the depths of their entire being.

Jesus was a passionate person. He didn't just engage the Pharisees in measured, polite debate; he challenged them, calling them hypocrites and a brood of vipers (Matthew 3:7; 12:34; 23:33). He didn't just quietly ask the Temple vendors to reconsider what they were doing; he overturned their tables, raging with a whip that they had turned God's house into a den of robbers (Matthew 21:12-13; John 2:13-16). Jesus was full of passion, which makes following in the Jesus way a passionate endeavor. It isn't easy. It's not for wimps. It's not about celebrating the joy of Easter every Sunday; it's filled with Maundy Thursdays and Good Fridays. It's intense.

We can see the intensity of the Jesus way in Luke 22. Jesus goes with his disciples to the garden to pray. He has finished his last meal with his followers and is in need of some time alone. Jesus asks the disciples to pray that they might not be tempted (or as some translations say, that they might not enter into a time of trial). He then moves off by himself and begins to pray, "Father, if you are willing, please take this cup of suffering away from me. Yet I want your will, not mine" (Luke 22:42, NLT). In his humanity, Jesus was struggling. It was taking everything he had to come to grips with what lay before him. The struggle was so great: "He was in such agony of spirit that his sweat fell to the ground like great drops of blood" (Luke 22:44, NLT).

Following in the Jesus way is not easy. It isn't about getting what you want—not even for Jesus himself. In the garden, Jesus was pleading with God, "Do you have a 'Plan B'? Can you think of some other way?" That sounds a lot like most of us. "God, this is what I'm facing; do you have a 'Plan B'? Can you think of some other future that doesn't involve having to go through this? Can you take this cup away?" So often we want a God who will soften the blow of our failures. I'm sure I am not the only one who has prayed for a life without pain. "Please, God, take this away from me. Protect me and keep me out of harm's way. Make my children's lives safe and secure."

We can't just celebrate the joy of Easter every Sunday and still follow in the Jesus way. We've got to experience sleepless nights. Jesus was experiencing a sleepless night in the garden. I've experienced sleepless nights, but usually I assume it's because something is wrong. My assumption is that I shouldn't have sleepless nights.

The reality, however, is that following in the Jesus way with passion, becoming a passionate person for Jesus, involves losing sleep. If we are following Jesus side by side, we will have sleepless nights, and we will also experience the unexpected. As Christ followers, we often have certain preconceived notions about how life is supposed to be: If we do our part and play by the rules, life should turn out a certain way. The disciples felt the same way. They had been following Jesus for three years. They had left their jobs, their homes, everything they had. They had certain expectations about how the future was going to turn out; after all, Jesus was the Messiah. They had witnessed his miracles and healings, they had heard him preach and teach. He was the real deal. Now they were going to Jerusalem for Passover. What an exciting time this would be! But then they got this news from Jesus himself: "When we get to Jerusalem . . . the Son of

Man will be betrayed to the leading priests and the teachers of religious law. They will sentence him to die and hand him over to the Romans" (Mark 10:33, NLT). *Great. That's not what we expected.* "They will mock him, spit on him, beat him with their whips, and kill him" (Mark 10:34, NLT). *Wonderful. We can't wait to get there.*

As we enter Holy Week, we all need to read about the last week of Jesus' life on earth. What happened is not what the disciples expected; and if we didn't know the story so well, it's probably not what we would have expected. From the beginning, it stunk. The betrayal stunk; the trial stunk. The disciples did what they never dreamed they would do: desert Jesus in his greatest time of need. To make matters worse, God was silent. Jesus, however, slips something in when he is telling the disciples about their upcoming weekend. He's almost sneaky in the way he tacks it on at the end: "but after three days [the Son of Man] will rise again" (Mark 10:34, NLT, adapted). I think most of us are in favor of a God who brings people back from the dead. That's our kind of God. Our problem is that we don't always want God practicing on us. We want to skip the pain part. We prefer to pass over the death thing. Let's just get right on to the eternal life part.

But that's not the Jesus way. God doesn't *dispense* with death. God *resurrects* us from it. The truth is that the Jesus way isn't about God taking pain *away* from God's people; it's about God providing us with strength, courage, and meaning, with abundant life, often in the *midst* of pain. We prefer to have no doubt, but God doesn't make our doubt disappear; instead God gives us faith to cover our doubt.

Paul described what the Jesus way is all about in Philippians— really knowing Christ and experiencing the mighty power that raised him from the dead (Philippians 3:10). That message appeals to us; but what Paul says next throws us off: "I can learn what it means to suffer with him, sharing in his death, so that, somehow, I can experience the resurrection from the dead!" (Philippians 3:10-11, NLT). When we read this passage, our reaction may be, "Who signed me up for this team?" But that is what being on Jesus' team is all about, sharing in his death so that we can experience resurrection—life. The reality of the Jesus way is that it is passionate—it goes all the way. Thus, if want to experience the power of God's resurrection, we must first be willing to embrace the pain.

Embracing the pain of the Crucifixion in order to experience the power of the Resurrection involves right living, not easy living. Jesus

75

prayed the same way we all pray when we're faced with something bad in our lives—when we discover we have cancer, when we lose a job, when we suddenly find ourselves a single parent, we all pray, *Please, if there's any way, take this cup—this burden—away from me.*

But life doesn't come from removing cups. When he was praying, Jesus added the biggest "but" of all time: "But God, it's not what I want, it's what you want." That's the key question: *What do you want? I know what I want, God, but what do you want?*

We all know what we want. I know what I want. I want health and happiness for my family; I want my marriage to be good and strong; I want to have a comfortable income, contribute something to my community, maybe even to the world. But those wants don't add up to passionate living. Jesus shows us passionate living: a God who becomes human and then gets crucified—for each one of us. You can't get more passionate than that; that's an everything-I've-got kind of commitment. The amazing thing for me as I meditate on Jesus' passion is that he didn't bail out. I find that remarkable. It would have been a huge temptation for me to drop the whole project, especially when everyone else did. It's easy to do something when you're surrounded by a group doing the same thing, but when you're on your own—the way Jesus was—that's another thing altogether. He didn't abandon the whole project; he didn't quit; he didn't run; he stuck with the future God had laid before him.

We all have times when our lives are filled with frustration, heartache, despair. Jesus understands all of that because he experienced it. But he didn't allow those experiences to stop him. He stayed focused on who he was and the reason he was here. He was deeply tapped into the source of his life and energy—"My nourishment comes from doing the will of God, who sent me, and from finishing his work" (John 4:34, NLT). Even at his most desperate moment, when he cried out, "My God, my God, why have you forsaken me?" (Mark 15:34, NLT), even then, Jesus kept his direction. We have all experienced God's absence, when we felt as though God was nowhere to be found. Jesus, in the midst of such doubt, kept his direction.

Michael Slaughter once described the amazing truth of Jesus' passion, saying, "God would rather go to hell for you than go to heaven without you." That is passion; that's whole-life commitment. That is the passion of the God in whose image we have been created; and because we are made in God's image, we've got a propensity for passion as well. God didn't make us for tepid living, lukewarm or in the middle; we were made for total commitment. God desires to be in relationship with you, a relationship that is more than a donation, more than a weekly ritual, more than something you do at a distance. God wants *all* of you. God wants the kind of commitment that compels you to be in the thick of things, to do whatever it takes in order that God might work in you and through you. That's the kind of dedication that accepts no excuses—a whole-life commitment. Passion is about blood, sweat, and tears; it means no holding back, giving it all.

The Via Dolorosa, which means "the way of the cross," is in the old city of Jerusalem. It is basically unchanged since the day Jesus walked it, carrying his cross to the place of his execution. The Via Dolorosa is made up of winding narrow streets and is filled with vendors who hawk their wares just as they did in Jesus' time. When I was thirteen, I visited Jerusalem, and we followed the Way of the Cross. It was a surreal experience for me. I noticed all the signs along the way proclaiming that this was the way that Jesus took to his crucifixion; yet people were going about their business, carrying groceries, kids playing in the street. At the time of my visit, the execution site itself overlooked a bus station. It was loud and smelly. As I walked, I thought, *Does anybody really* get *it? Does anyone really understand what it means to walk the way of the cross?*

That question is as real for me now as it was thirty years ago, because that's Jesus' invitation to each of us. "If any of you wants to be my follower, you must put aside your selfish ambition, shoulder your cross, and follow me" (Matthew 16:24, NLT). Following Jesus involves sacrifice; it can be painful, because the kingdom of Jesus is ruled not from a throne but from a cross. So many people hear this message, but so few act on it. It's those who do act, people of passion, who change the world. The apostle Paul said, "I have been crucified with Christ" (Galatians 2:19, NLT). It's not about following at a distance; it's about a whole-life commitment. Paul said, "I myself no longer live, but Christ lives in me" (Galatians 2:20, NLT). I will do whatever it takes so that God can work in me and through me. I will do anything, even when there's pain, even when it feels as though God is nowhere to be found, even when the diagnosis is not good, even when my spouse walks out, even when . . . I will walk side by side; I will give everything I have, because Jesus gave me everything he is.

In his letter to the Roman church, Paul wrote, "I consider that the sufferings of this present time are not worth comparing with the glory about to be revealed to us" (Romans 8:18, NRSV). Moving into the light of the fire takes passion. It's about blood, sweat, and tears. It's not for wimps. The fire can be hot and the journey long. But it is the journey to which our Lord Jesus calls us; and it is a journey that provides immense rewards, both now and into eternity.

Lance Armstrong won his first Tour de France in 1999. The Tour is one of the most prestigious races in cycling, so Armstrong's victory was significant. Even more significant was the fact that his victory came on the heels of his successful battle with testicular cancer that had spread into his lungs and brain. While Armstrong is not a Christan, and like all of us is far from perfect, there is no doubt that his journey to the Tour was long and arduous, filled with roadblocks and detours, blood, sweat, and tears. As it would for any of us, those difficulties made his 1999 victory sweet indeed.

The following year, at the 2000 Tour de France, Armstrong was not expected to win despite his impressive showing in 1999. Some of the world's other leading cyclists had been disqualified from the 1999 race but were now back and ready to compete. The course was more challenging in 2000 as well, so few people held much hope for an Armstrong victory; yet in a stunning finish, he claimed first place, a full six minutes ahead of his competition. In 2004, after living through the intensity of cancer, following a road of hardship and difficulty, and single-mindedly giving his all for his sport, Lance Armstrong won an unprecedented sixth consecutive Tour de France victory.

As we move ever closer to Easter and beyond, I pray that you would continue to follow Jesus, up close and in the thick of things. I pray that you would feel the passion, continue to single-mindedly give your all to God, and experience the victory of God's whole life commitment for you. In her famous play-cycle, *The Man Born to Be King*, written for the BBC, Dorothy Sayers wrote:

[The disciples] had seen the strong hands of God twist the crown of thorns into a crown of glory, and in hands as strong as that they knew themselves safe. They had misunderstood practically everything Christ had ever said to them, but no matter: the thing made sense at last, and the meaning was far beyond anything they had dreamed. They had expected a walkover, and they beheld a victory; they had expected an earthly Messiah, and they beheld the Soul of Eternity (from *The Man Born to Be King*, in "The Triumph of Easter," by Dorothy L. Sayers, as cited in *Christianity Today*, Vol. 41, No. 4).

I pray that in following Jesus side by side, you might come to know the joy of his victory; that in carrying your cross as he did, you might experience new life as he did; that in standing close to the fire, you might behold the Soul of Eternity.

Study / Discussion Questions

1. How have you experienced the observance of Palm Sunday, this year or in the past? How has an understanding of Jesus' Passion, his sufferings, fit into that experience?

2. Have you ever had a "garden experience," where you pled with God for a "Plan B"? If so, describe that experience. If not, reflect on or discuss the experience of someone close to you who has gone through such an experience.

3. Reflect on / discuss a time when, rather than dispensing with the pain, God provided you the resources to persevere through it.

4. The author describes whole-life commitment in this declaration: "I will walk side by side; I will give everything I have, because Jesus gave me everything he is." Having experienced this study, what commitments do you feel you need to make to begin "walking side by side" with Jesus? What do you need to give to God in response to Jesus' giving everything he is to you?

Focus for the Coming Week

Reflect on God's whole-life commitment for you, the passionate giving of Godself on your behalf. Bring Jesus' sacrifice clearly before you in order to experience fully the significance of his passion. Then, having immersed yourself in Jesus' dying, move toward your celebration of Easter with excitement and joy, knowing that having been crucified with Christ, Christ now lives within you, and you will be raised with him in glory.

Prayer

Lord Jesus, thank you for being willing to make a total-life commitment for me. Thank you for your passion. Holy Spirit of Jesus, enervate my heart that I might be passionate as you are, that I might be empowered to go all the way with the all-of-me commitment you desire. Please forgive me when I drop back to a distance, living out a lukewarm faith that is not fully engaged. Give me eyes to see the life-giving power of your resurrection, even in the midst of my own challenges, suffering, and pain, that in dying with you, I might truly know you and experience the power that raised you from the dead. Amen.